Escape to the *Sea*

Tom Sullivan A.B.

Edited by Mike Starke

Whittles Publishing

Published by
Whittles Publishing,
Dunbeath,
Caithness KW6 6EY,
Scotland, UK
www.whittlespublishing.com

Frontispiece: Tom Sullivan pictured around the time of writing his memoirs

Printed and bound in the United Kingdom by Severn, Gloucester

MIX
Paper from
responsible sources
FSC
www.fsc.org   FSC® C022174

To Sue

"She is foremost of those that I would hear praised.
I have gone about the house, gone up and down
As a man does who has published a new book,
Or a young girl dressed out in her new gown."
W. B. Yeats

Contents

Acknowledgements

As I clambered through the branches of my family tree to learn more about Thomas Sullivan Green, firm handholds were provided by these relatives, to whom I owe a great debt of gratitude.

In alphabetical order: Mo Goulding, Judith Hoad, the Rev Terence Knight, John Starke, Peter Starke, Kay Walden, and Patrick Starke for his illustrations of ships' rigs.

Thanks also to John Leath, whose expert help and steadfast encouragement, spanning two decades, were invaluable.

For taking the trouble to answer queries into the minutiae of Thomas Sullivan Green's life, I am indebted to Alan A. Morton and Alan Standley, as well as the helpful records staff of Gwent County Council and Bristol City Council, among numerous others whose seemingly small contributions have added together to enhance the larger picture.

Without the faith of Dr Keith Whittles, of Whittles Publishing, and his team, Thomas Sullivan Green's dream of his memoirs being published would not have been realised, so his and my gratitude go to them.

Above all, I thank my wife, Sue, not only for her tireless dedication to transcribing my edited manuscript, but also for her boundless support during the triumphs and tribulations of the quest for my great-grandfather.

Mike Starke
Chale Green

Foreword

I am the family face;
Flesh perishes, I live on.

— Thomas Hardy

Tracking down ancestors is like hosting an elaborate family reunion with a longer guest list than usual. The list is so long because those bidden to the feast of nostalgia are to be found on both sides of the grave. What is most intriguing for the host of such an event is that, in extending invitations back several generations, new branches of the family tree are discovered with living roots spreading down to the present day.

I was first spurred on to organise my own family reunion some years ago in order to try to get to know better one man that I wanted to be the guest of honour. For no gathering of my far-flung relatives ever took place without the exploits of my great-grandfather, Thomas Sullivan Green, being brought to mind by someone.

Some said he was a runaway who fled to sea in a sailing ship. To others he was the illegitimate son of an Irish aristocrat, banished with his abandoned mother to his fate in England. Another version had him as a merchant adventurer, trading with the natives in the trackless backwoods of Africa. Then there were those who believed he had been an orphan of the Irish potato famines of the 1840s, packed off by desperate parents as a teenager to eke out a bare survival on the land in South Wales.

It was obvious that he could not be all of these things. I set out to tease the strands of truth from this richly woven tapestry of family fantasy. I was to find that fact was as fascinating as the fictions.

I cajoled relatives into recounting their personal recollections of Thomas Sullivan Green. Thus one of the first discoveries was that he was universally known as Jack Green. The use of an alias already hinted at a whiff of exotic spice. Then a series of events unfolded which were to bring me as close to knowing the man as if he were a flesh-and-blood guest at a family reunion.

Hearing of my quest for my great-grandfather, but not knowing where I lived, a distant cousin wrote from her home in County Cork, Eire, to my sister in County Donegal. Was I aware, our cousin asked, that the old man had written his memoirs of his experiences as a seaman in Victorian times? The letter then went on to stretch coincidence into what could be considered the luck of the Irish by saying that the manuscript had last been heard of in the possession of a branch of our far-flung family thought to live in Portsmouth, just a ferry ride away from my Isle of Wight home.

I was soon armed with the knowledge that another great grandson of Thomas Sullivan Green was then the Rural Dean of Portsmouth. I quickly discovered a telephone number to match the name.

"I am either going to be rather embarrassed or saying hello to a long-lost relative," I told the voice that answered the phone.

"Try me," replied the unruffled clergyman. I did, and he was able to greet me with: "Hello, cousin."

With growing excitement I learned that not only did my new-found relative have the manuscript I sought but he also had a wealth of other documents which were to shed light on the life of our great-grandfather.

A few days later I found myself in my cousin's book-lined study poring over the fading papers. And there lay the object of my quest: a box containing 200 fine-lined loose leaves, aged to the colour of the Scotch and water with which we toasted our long-overdue meeting.

The pages were covered in bold, flowing handwriting with a confident, forward slope to it. The top sheet bore the words:

At Sea under Canvas
Fifty Years Ago
By "Tom Sullivan"

Then pencilled and underlined beneath the name came the afterthought: AB – Able Bodied seaman.

I savoured the old salt's yarns and pictured the writer holding us spellbound at my imaginary family reunion with his tales of the bygone days of deep sea sail. But here was not just a fragment of family history. Here too was a unique record of an ordinary man's recollections of everyday life and work in Victorian Britain.

His descriptions of ports of call and cargoes give a first-hand view of what made trade prosper in a remarkable period of the nation's history. Just as intriguing is the character of the man, which comes through the narrative with the telling snatches of dialogue.

The very pen strokes of the original manuscript have a bold, assertive slope indicating an individual of some self-confidence and determination. The fact that he believed his tale worth telling points to the same trait. It was apparent that here was a remarkable man.

Remarkable people are expected to fall into the three time-honoured categories of those who are born to greatness, those who achieve greatness and those who have greatness thrust upon them. Many never even reach the foothills of these three lofty peaks. However, among them are some truly remarkable people, too.

Such a person was Thomas Sullivan Green, who also adopted the alias Jack Green to escape detection by the authorities during one of the seafaring adventures that are the subject of this autobiographical narrative. This name stayed with him to the end of his long life, although he reverted to 'Tom Sullivan' as author of his reminiscences.

Escape to the Sea, as Tom's memoirs have been re-christened, deals only with the years he spent before the mast under sail. It was his intention to describe the life and times of a seaman below decks aboard the merchant vessels that plied the seven seas to satisfy the insatiable appetite for raw materials of the industrial machine at the heart of Queen Victoria's British Empire.

In concentrating on his experiences as a merchant mariner, he hoped his words would "be both instructive and amusing, especially to the youths and lads who are still going to school". It is known that he was keen to have his work published to encourage young men to take up a career at sea, as he had done.

But this was only part of Jack Green's eventful life. What helped mould his remarkable character was what went before, and his new ventures after he "swallowed the anchor" to come ashore and settle down at last with his own family had remarkable features about them, too.

Thomas Sullivan Green was born in London on 2 March 1846. His father, John, had been a tailor in or around the city of Cork but had been forced to flee his native Ireland when the poverty induced by the potato famine struck his trade as the knock-on effect of his customers being unable to afford his wares. The impoverished immigrant family's plight was only to get worse after they settled in the Seven Dials area of the capital – now, ironically, part of the fashionable tourist attraction that is Covent Garden and Neal Street.

In the 1840s, the area was known as the stews: an area of squalid slums in airless streets that scarcely saw the light of day through the city's smoke-laden murk. Disease was rife, and none more so than cholera, which thrived in the filth of the cramped tenements with no clean water for their occupants to drink. One of the epidemics of the killer disease claimed the infant Tom's parents, who both died when he was only two years old. He always believed that he had a sister who also survived, and he made strenuous but ultimately vain efforts to track her down throughout his long life.

He takes up his own story at the point of being orphaned, but, tantalisingly, he does not explain the fine detail of how he came to be well educated and apprenticed to a man in his father's trade of tailoring. There is anecdotal evidence to suggest he might have been taken under the wing of family friends or colleagues among the tailoring fraternity, for it is unlikely an infant Irish immigrant orphan would have survived without a good deal of care and attention, apart from the anonymous "authorities" to whom he refers. At any event, it was Tom's good fortune that there were benefactors in the offing, although their names remain a mystery.

He acknowledged that he had a good education. The fact he could write so eloquently about his experiences, plus his obvious head for figures – described as both a boon and a bane on one ship – and his musical aptitude all show that he must have been a willing and adept student.

His eventually fortunate early life could have been very different. Even if he had survived infancy, he might have faced the dubious prospect of "living off the parish" as a workhouse boy, like Dickens's Oliver Twist. An unpromising start for anyone. An apprenticeship, or something by that name, might have been chosen for him, and even worse slavery than he claimed to have encountered could have been his fate.

The young sailor's exploits, with all their trials and triumphs, are a far cry from the ghastly environment of his early youth. Many might think that he would have done well to stick to the tailoring trade, and that his sudden departure from it after five of seven years was foolhardy, but he saw it as his escape, and that escape was to the sea that he came to love – although he retained the skill to make clothes and was renowned in later years for sewing his own three-piece suits and garments for his family.

The remarkable is apparent, again, as his tale unfolds. The life of a Victorian seaman is extraordinary enough by comparison with 21st-century conditions of employment. But Tom, or Jack, as he becomes, has the equally remarkable good fortune to stumble across some historic events. He gives a vivid first-hand account of seeing the plight of the freed slaves in the aftermath of the American Civil War. Then there is the horrific eye-witness account of a public hanging in Stafford – the last to take place there, according to official records. He witnesses lurid and exotic happenings while a member of trading ships' crews on the west African coast and is commanded by the best and worst of captains the merchant navy issued with masters' tickets.

There is evidence that his use of the alias John or Jack Green came about as a stratagem to avoid trouble with the authorities. I believe he adopted the pseudonym when he deserted a ship that he feared was not seaworthy, thus breaching the articles binding him to the vessel's crew for the duration of a voyage. This was deemed a serious crime punishable by imprisonment. Was his adoption of the name John a gesture towards his dead father who bore that name? I'm sure psychologists might argue it spoke of a young man's need to somehow fill the void where the parent he never really knew should have been.

The name John Green is used consistently on the Certificates of Discharge from ships spanning the 20 or so years my great-grandfather spent going to sea. He is also addressed as "Mr Jack Green" in an interview with the *Bristol Times* in May 1926 (see Appendix A). Yet he used his real name when he wrote in the frontispiece of his family Bible, when in January 1874, at the age of 27 he married Mary Ann Kinsey, a dressmaker, and when he wrote his will towards the end of his long life. To cap it all, he hides behind a third combination of his names as a nom de plume for his memoirs: Tom Sullivan.

In a world fraught with uncertainties for one of Tom's class and upbringing, it is significant he seems to have developed cunning as a tool of self-preservation, covering his tracks with an alias when he found himself falling foul of those in authority. Alongside his cunning went resourcefulness. Hungry and homeless, he set his self-taught musical talents on a German concertina to work in his early career to earn enough for food and lodging. He shows he was every inch a survivor.

He goes to some pains to let his readers know he was not afraid to take on captains he served under. There is a streak of stubborn defiance here that, while a key to Tom's survival, probably made him a difficult shipmate to get on with at times. There is no question that he liked to get his own way, willy nilly, among his peers, too. Not for him a reasoned argument on the pros and cons of rowdy gambling among fellow crew members on one voyage. Tom pitches the offenders' playing cards into the galley stove, and that's that.

Like any young man of spirit, he could be cocky to the point of insolence. His account of a conversation with a Jewish pawnbroker, while undoubtedly reflecting contemporary attitudes, shows him subjecting the shopkeeper to racial taunts. Elsewhere he revels in an African getting a tongue-lashing from a shipmate. And yet he also shows compassion and admiration for American and African blacks, which might not have been shared by many of his contemporaries in days when racial tolerance was, to many, an unheard of concept in a world where the sun never set on the dominions of the British Queen Empress.

Among Tom's particular saving graces was his humour. This shines through his narrative, especially in the snatches of dialogue he manages to recall miraculously word-perfect after half a century. But perhaps there was enough of the tailor in him to know his well-spun yarn was the better for being plied with strands of direct speech? Not unnaturally, Tom gives himself the last word in most of these exchanges. Many are used to illustrate incidents which amused him at the time.

His good humour, with a hint of his cocky irreverence, must have been what prompted him to play a game of pickpocket with his grandchildren in the 1920s. One of his granddaughters recalls how the old man would stroll up his garden path in Bedminster, Bristol, inviting her and her young siblings – squealing with delight – to creep up and pick sweets from his pockets while he pretended not to notice. I can imagine the old man's impish grin as scowling mothers – his own daughters – scolded him for teaching the youngsters thieving ways. And to their parental exasperation, he would stuff his pockets with sweets again: a feigned Fagin leading his retinue of Artful Dodgers up the garden path once more.

While my great-grandfather's memoirs give a good deal of information about him and his life at sea, it is by no means the whole picture. He deliberately deals only with that part of his life spent as a sailor. He indicated to his family when he was alive that he would like to have seen his account published so he could share his love of the sea with others. His narrative chronicles his early years, followed by a succession of voyages interspersed with brief periods ashore, but this represents only a small part of his long and varied life.

From official and family documents, as well as personal recollections of relatives, I have been able to build up a picture of the life and times of Thomas Sullivan Green. Often the schooling of pauper orphans was left to those unfit – usually through mental illness – for other duties in the workhouse, so Tom was fortunate indeed to have received the good education he clearly had and for which he expressed gratitude. However, his luck was not to last, and his apprenticeship to a tailor at 14 – two years after many of the youngsters of his time were taken on – seems to have been more in keeping with the harsh regime expected of the system at the time.

Child apprentices were set to work in appalling conditions for long hours; often in the guardianship of unspeakably cruel masters. Reformers met fierce official resistance to even the most modest attempts to improve the lot of child labourers. Legislation to reduce children's hours of work to 10 a day from as much as 19 was consistently blocked by a Parliament made up largely of men benefiting from this near-slavery.

My great-grandfather took the law into his own hands and put and end to his own drudgery by running away to sea at 19 after five of his seven years as an apprentice. It apparently took him some time to pluck up the courage for his desperate act. For, romantic as it may seem to us to set out to seek one's fortune in an elegant sailing vessel, such a course of action was fraught with perils for a Victorian teenager and would not have been undertaken lightly. Young Tom was setting his face against the authorities that had become his surrogate parents, and put himself beyond the pale with his apprentice master.

While he perceived the life of a merchant mariner as his "escape" from the apparently tyrannical tailor, it offered the even-harsher task masters of wind and waves. There was also the uncertain prospect of being subject to the whims of sometimes-capricious skippers whose authority as sea was second only to God's, as he was soon to find out.

Just a year after going to sea he decided to break another apprenticeship to escape the threat of violence at the hands of a bullying skipper. He expresses no regret, but this cost him the career prospect of becoming an officer and eventually master of his own ship. Although a man of evident intelligence and ability, he shows little professional ambition. Perhaps, like Oscar Wilde, he could dismiss it cynically as "the last refuge of failure". Despite the occasional thumbing of his nose in the direction of the quarter deck, "John Green's" Certificates of Discharge consistently show his ability and conduct earn the top rating of "Very Good".

He clearly relished life under sail as opposed to being propelled through the water by the new-fangled steamships. Even the sight of the historic Brunel vessel, the *Great Eastern*, in Cork's Queenstown harbour, now Cobh, early in 1867 is marred for him by the observation that she was making a great "smother" of smoke.

Landfalls in exotic parts of the world were intriguing to his inquiring mind. The detailed descriptions he gives of foreign ports and their people convince me that he revelled in each new experience. His recollections remained sharp enough for him to commit them to paper half a century later when he was in his seventies.

This eye-witness account of a young man's life in Victorian times not only gives a unique insight into the everyday preoccupations of a sailor under canvas, but also a first-hand view of significant events of national and international importance. The 20-year-old seafarer's horror at stumbling across the bungled public execution of the murderer William Collier in Stafford in 1866 (see Appendix C) conjures up a vivid picture from the pages of British history: the last public execution in Staffordshire before abolition.

On a voyage to Savannah, Georgia, later the same year and shortly after the devastating war between the states, the young sailor describes the human misery that resulted from the scorched earth campaigns of the Union General, William Tecumseh Sherman. The young seaman is moved by the plight of the emancipated slaves suffering unbearable hardships following the defeat of the Confederacy.

The time for travelling the world had to stop for young "Jack" when he found himself a job ashore, met and married Mary Ann Kinsey, one year his junior, and "swallowed the anchor" – for a time, at least – when he was in his late twenties. His bride was brought up in the hamlet of Trelleck Grange in the beautiful Wye Valley. Mary Ann, later to be known as "Aunt Polly" by her family in Trelleck, was born in Gedney Hill near the Lincolnshire market town of Holbeach. Her father, Edward, a labourer, died when she and her two brothers were young and her mother, Ann, travelled across the country to Trellick Grange. Why is not clear. Maybe relatives were there.

Ann made her living as a travelling dressmaker, taking her skills to outlying farms and more remote villages. Although skilled with her hands, she could not read or write. Mary Ann's name is written in Jack Green's hand on their marriage certificate, dated 25 January 1874, with her mark "X" after it.

Clues from Jack Green's own narrative and other official documentary fragments point to his having had an intriguing romantic involvement. In the autumn of 1867 the 21-year-old Jack was on the run after jumping the ship bound for Naples that he had signed to serve on. He evaded capture and got rid of his sailor's garb, for if he had been captured he could have expected severe treatment.

Although "disguised", he must have felt wary and vulnerable when he set off for Bristol, a city he had never been to before. On the way he accepts the recommendation of a pub landlord in Whitchurch, a man he had only met for a few minutes while waiting for a train, and seeks out an unmarried boarding-house keeper in Jacob's Well. In retrospect, he writes scathingly about her duplicity in money matters. But this did not stop him returning to her time and again between voyages for no less than five years.

Could it be that he was providing rather more towards the housekeeping than a mere tenant might be expected to and that his later accusations were born of the jealous fury of a jilted lover? Indeed, had this mystery woman been as dishonest and ill-disposed towards Jack as he indicates, it is highly likely that the guilty secret of his desertion would not have stayed secret long.

Jack makes no mention in his memoirs of his own wedding in 1874, but he makes sure we know his Bristol landlady in 1872 during one of his absences. There is no date in the text for Jack's interlude ashore in Chepstow (see Chapter 13) but it would seem to have been just after his landlady's marriage as he went job-hunting at the early workings on the Severn Tunnel, which began in 1873. Trellick Grange, where Jack's wife-to-be lived, is not far from Chepstow and it is easy to imagine that he might have met her then. Perhaps the draper he fell out with was the one who supplied Mary Ann's mother with material for her dressmaking trade. Although Jack dismisses his description of the episode in Chepstow, as a grocer's warehouseman, as a "shore-going venture" between voyages, it is likely he "swallowed the anchor" for rather longer than he suggests.

Clearly he did not last long in Chepstow, but long enough to woo Mary Ann, whom he wed in Bristol. On their marriage certificate he is described as a grocer and family

Tom Sullivan lovingly inscribed his six children's names in the family Bible in his distinctive hand. His wife, Mary Ann, could not write

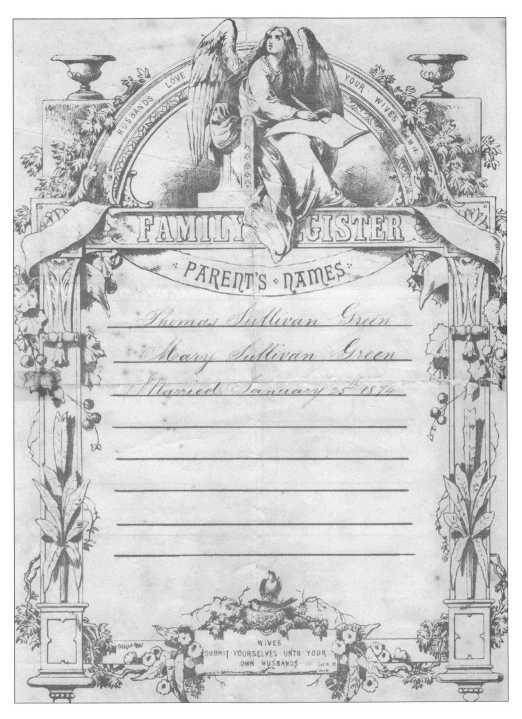

Tom Sullivan appears to have signed up himself and his spouse to the Victorian values at the head and foot of this Bible plate. Meanwhile, perhaps the angel is raising a despairing eye to Heaven over the misplaced apostrophe printed beneath her

records indicate he had his own shop at one time. Some recall seeing papers showing that Jack had taken out a patent on a cheese slicing device for use in shops.

Jilted Jack and Mary Ann wasted no time in starting a family, and Amy Sullivan Green was born in November, nine months and nine days after the wedding day. Their sole son, Harold, was born nearly two years later, the only other child to retain Sullivan in the name. Beatrice Green came along two years after that. It was Beatrice who looked after Jack in his old age at her home in Southville, Bristol. Another two-year gap followed before Gertrude was born. She did not survive childhood.

In 1883, Jack set sail again for a final fling at sea. Obviously drawing on his experiences in the grocery trade, he took berths as ship's steward and cook. The last two voyages were short and occupied just under a year. My own grandmother, Mary, was born on 29 September 1884. This indicates a particularly fond farewell having been made by Jack and Mary Ann just days before the start of his last signing-on, on 5 February that year. The family was completed with the addition of Frances Minnie in 1886, two years after Mary in the family's biennial birth pattern.

Jack now "swallowed the anchor" for good, in his mid-thirties. Later he is thought to have become an innkeeper briefly before being taken on as a clerk at Bristol's Ashton Gate Brewery. He rose to be a manager before his retirement. But even this final chapter

The marriage certificate of Thomas Sullivan Green and Mary Ann Kinsey. Note the bride signed with an "X"

of his working life was not without incident. Relatives recall that he fell out with the firm shortly before he was due to retire and left in high dudgeon without his pension – shades of earlier examples of his "cutting off his nose to spite his face", as with the Scottish skipper at Poole.

His daughter Beatrice married a sailor in the Royal Navy. How it must have gladdened the old salt Jack Green's heart when their son, Donald John Sullivan Eastman, followed in his father's footsteps by going to Greenwich Naval School at the age of 11. How it must have broken his heart, too, when Donald died of tuberculosis in the Haslar Royal Naval Hospital, Gosport, when he was only 21.

A few months later, on 13 November 1932, Thomas Sullivan "Jack" Green died too, aged 86. It was a tragic irony for one who had lived long and actively that both the beginning and the end of his life had been marked by the death of his nearest and dearest as a result of disease.

Thomas Sullivan Green was buried in the same grave as his wife, whom he had survived by 19 years, and his

*Mike Starke at the family grave in
Greenbank cemetery, Bristol*

grandson, Donald. His firstborn, Amy, was to join him there in 1958 when she died, aged 84.

It is known my great-grandfather married again in old age. His bride was Kate Reynold and she bore him a daughter, Edith. They have been obscured from view in the family annals by the sulphurous fumes of disapproval that tend to cloud such late-in-life unions.

One last document remains in the old man's own hand: his will. Some of the flourish of his memoirs manuscript has gone, but there is still the assertive slope to the handwriting on the half sheet of lined exercise book paper. It is addressed from Beatrice's home in Birch Road, Southville, Bristol, but is undated. It reads:

> *The last will of me, Thomas Sullivan Green, in which I give all that belongs to me to my daughters, Amy and Beatrice, who will kindly engage Mr Hodges (undertaker) to take me, when the breath is out of my body, to Greenbank (cemetery) without any ceremony whatever.*

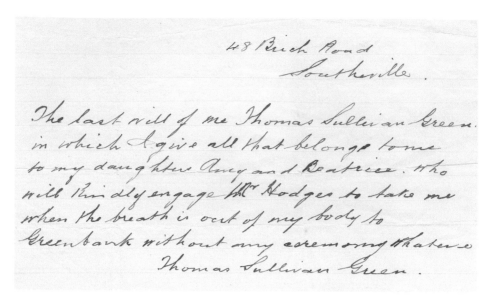

Tom Sullivan Green's handwritten will

He could not resist one last gesture of defiance by thumbing his nose at the sober convention of funeral pomp.

Editor's Note

I have kept the editing of these memoirs to a minimum in order to preserve the individual, vibrant style of my great-grandfather, Thomas Sullivan Green. Obviously I had to change the original title since the very least amendment would have made it At *Sea under Canvas One Hundred and Thirty Years Ago*. I also added the quotations that head each chapter. I trust the crusty old salt, a well-read man, by all accounts, would not disapprove.

Now it's time for us to join the man himself. Allow me to introduce you to Thomas Sullivan Green, alias Tom Sullivan, alias Jack Green … AB

Mike Starke
Chale Green, Isle of Wight

Tom Sullivan's ports of call in and around the British Isles

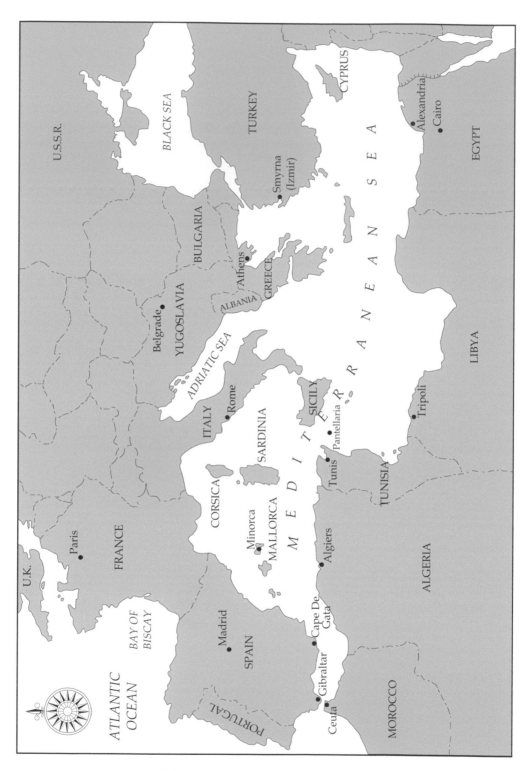

Tom Sullivan's voyages took him to the Mediterranean

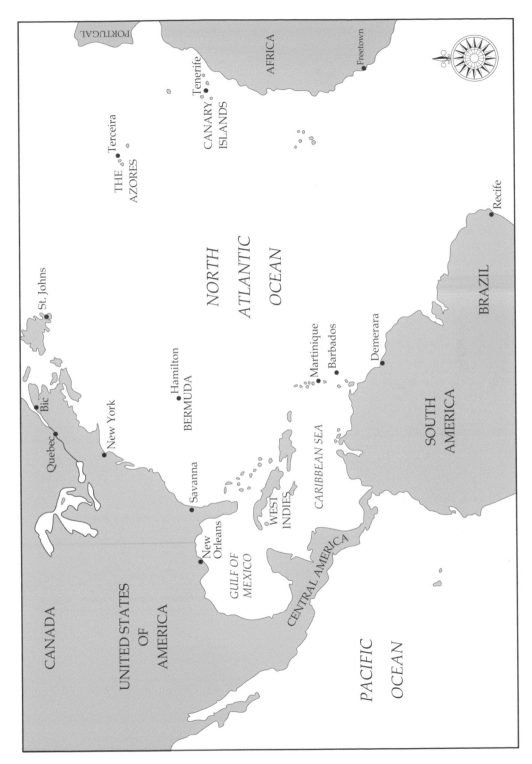

Trans–Atlantic trips to North and South America brought Tom Sullivan danger and excitement

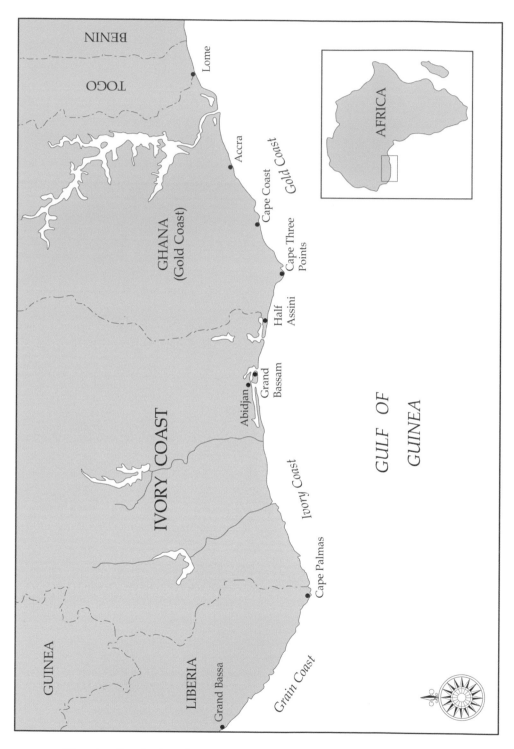

The palm oil trade along the West African coast was the respectable commercial replacement for the abolished slave trade

Prologue

Oh! Teach the orphan-boy to read,
Or teach the orphan-girl to sew.

— **Alfred Lord Tennyson**

I was two years of age when I lost both parents in London's great plague of cholera in 1848[1] and was taken in charge by the authorities.[2]

I was sent to one of the large schools just outside London, I having been born in that city, and a very fine school it was. Besides being well taught there, you also had the advantage of learning a good trade, which included every ordinary business by which you could earn your living.[3] We had one day at school and one at the workshop alternately. When I attained the age of 14 years, it was time to be apprenticed out to any tradesman who chose to make an application for a lad.

So it happened that one day a tailor (the trade I had learned) came to the school for a lad and I, being next in the books, I suppose, was sent off willy-nilly to London to be apprenticed for seven years.

---

1   Cholera, a virulent and often fatal infection contracted from contaminated water, plagued London in the 19th century. The outbreak of 1848–9 that claimed the lives of Tom's parents was particularly severe and resulted in 15,000 recorded deaths in the capital. London at the time had no electricity, there were cows and horses in the streets and general sanitation was poor. Waste matter from humans and beasts flowed through sewers and directly into the Thames, from which drinking water was pumped by the private water companies that supplied the city's householders. The idea that microbes in the contaminated water might be responsible for cholera was considered by experts at the time as, at best, fanciful. Unclean air was thought to be the culprit until epidemiologist John Snow made the link between the disease and water supplies.

2   Victorians liked nothing better than a biblical text, often taken out of context, to suit their prejudices. Thus Christ's words from St John's Gospel, "For the poor always ye have with you", formed the backcloth to their dealing with poverty, which some saw as vital to a prosperous society. The pamphleteer Patrick Colquhoun wrote earlier, in 1806:

> Poverty is a most necessary and indispensable ingredient in society. It is the lot of man. It is the source of wealth, since without poverty there would be no labour and without labour there could be no riches, no refinement, no comfort and no benefit to those who may be possessed of wealth.

Thus providing for the poor and setting them to work was enshrined in the Poor Law Amendment Act of 1834. This saw parish administration of the poor combined into Poor Law Unions, starting with London. These might have been "the authorities" Tom describes, but his treatment does not seem to have been as harsh as an immigrant orphan might have expected in the workhouse. This leads to the belief that these authorities may have had something to do with his dead father's tailoring trade guild and his former colleagues. The biggest clue to this, perhaps, is that young Tom is eventually apprenticed to a tailor. He never lost the skills he learnt, as he is remembered as making his own three-piece suits at a ripe old age.

3   The orphan Tom was doubly fortunate in his education, too, which clearly developed his ability to write and, as he describes later, to be adept enough with mathematics to manage a ship's accounts.

I am sorry to say that I found the people and the place anything but what I had expected and had been given to understand they would be. I was made a sort of general servant and had to work from six in the morning until eight at night, badly clothed and half starved.

Anyway, I stayed there for five years out of the seven. Then it was that I thought of the sea as a way out of such a miserable life.

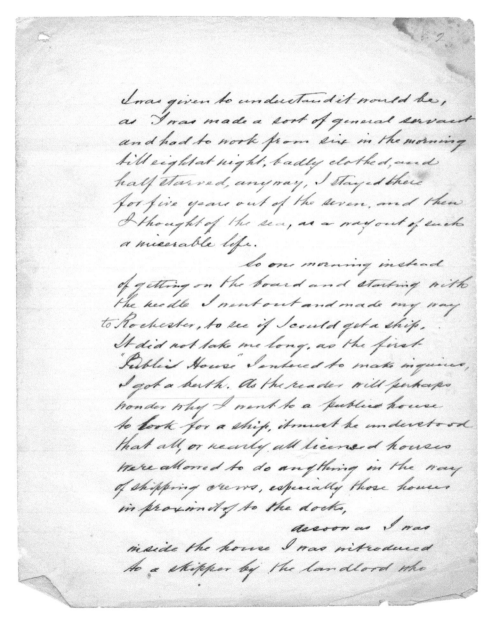

A page from Tom Sullivan's 200-page handwritten manuscript

1

When men come to like a sea life,
they are not fit to live on land.
— **Samuel Johnson**

S o one morning, instead of going on the board and starting with the needle, I went out and made my way to Rochester to see if I could get a ship.

It did not take me long, as the first public house I entered to make inquiries was where I got a berth. As the reader will perhaps wonder why I went to a public house to look for a ship, it must be understood that all – or nearly all – such houses were allowed to do anything in the way of shipping crews, especially those houses in close proximity to the docks.

As soon as I was inside the house I was introduced to a skipper by the landlord who had asked me what I wanted. He took me into the tap room where there were several captains seated around a table, with tankards of ale in front of them, chatting and smoking long pipes.

"Hello, my boy," says one of them. "Are you the lad that wants a ship?"

"Yes, captain," says I. "Do you require my services?"

"Come here," he says, "and let me have a look at you."

So, after a bit of a confab and as he seemed a very nice man who thought I would suit him, I agreed there and then to sign articles to go to West Hartlepool to be apprenticed to the owner for three years.[1]

"Now," says the skipper, "we had better get aboard and have something to eat and a look around, as we sail in the morning." So he handed me over to the mate whose watch it happened I was to be in.

---

1   These articles of indenture apprenticed Tom to the ship owner, and he could look forward to graduating to deck officer status in due course. He had already broken one set of articles, though, by fleeing from his tailoring master.

After having a good meal I was sent below where I soon made friends with the rest of the crew. As we had to sleep in hammocks, one of the crew took me in hand, showing me the way to sling it, as well as get into it. This can be rather a ticklish job, getting in one side and falling out the other, but I managed it at last and found there were more uncomfortable things to sleep in than hammocks.

Before we set sail in the morning, the skipper gave me some money and sent one of the crew with me to go ashore and get myself a rig-out which consisted of a mattress, blanket, plate, hookpot, pannikin and spoon. It was not a very elaborate outfit, but it was all I required until we got to West Hartlepool, our port of destination and where the owner lived.

The first morning at sea, the mate instructed one of the crew in our watch to show me all the easy jobs until I got my sea legs. I got on very well and before we got into port I was able to go aloft and take my turn at the wheel as well as the rest of the crew and do my share of the work. I thought it rather strange to find the sea had no effect on me as regards sickness, while the skipper, apparently, was sick every voyage he went on.

As soon as we arrived in port, I was taken to the owner for signing articles of apprenticeship. That gentleman was a butcher in a very large way of business, having made a lot of money running the blockade in the American Civil War.[2] He was very pleased to see me and when I was in his office signing articles he gave me a lot of good advice, as did the skipper, and as we were leaving he says: "Now, my lad, I expect you to be able to take charge and sail one of my ships the same as your captain here when you have finished your apprenticeship. So do your best and if you are a good lad and show a desire to get on I will see to your education."

Our vessel was a brig of 300 tons and was Nova Scotia-built of softwood, of which a great number were built in those days at the same yards. We had the best of food and plenty of it. I being the youngest apprentice, I had to take on the cooking which I soon got used to. It was rather hard work as I had to do deck work as well, lamp-trimming being part of my duties too. But notwithstanding all the work, I was very comfortable and happy, so it can be imagined how sorry I was to leave the ship for reasons given later.

The first few voyages I had were to the north of France; Dieppe, Dunkirk, Calais and so on, as it was winter and the Baltic frozen up. It was the custom of most coasters in those days to trade in the Baltic during the summer months and the Channel in the winter. As soon as the Baltic opened, our ship was one of about a dozen that set sail from Hartlepool for various ports there, we being bound for Gefle [Gävle] in the Gulf of Bothnia. This voyage was very interesting to me. We had fine weather the whole of the passage and I will never forget it.

After getting through the Sound and rounding the south coast of Sweden, we passed the island of Bornholm. Then quite a fleet of boats came alongside to do a bit of trading,

---

2   See Appendix B

offering a bucket of eggs for a bucket of coal, or two buckets of potatoes for one of coal, so we did a pretty good trade with them.

We arrived at our destination about two days after passing Bornholm and I thought when we got ashore that Gefle was the most delightful place it was possible to be in. Most of the inhabitants could speak good English and they gave us a very good time while we were there. There seemed to be no end to their hospitality. They would take us about after we finished work and show us all there was to be seen with an entertainment at one of their homes in the evening before we went back on board the ship.

Provisions were very cheap there. Butter was sixpence a pound, bacon the same price and eggs threepence a dozen,[3] all fresh from the farm. I was very much amused at the way they made and stored their bread. It was made from rye flour in the form of a plate with a hole in the middle through which a string was passed. About two dozen were strung thus and then hung up on hooks which were fastened to the rafters of the kitchen. I was told that bread so made and stored will keep for years. The cakes were about a quarter of an inch thick and eaten with plenty of butter.

Having finished loading, we sailed for West Hartlepool, I for one being sorry to leave Gefle where we were so kindly treated. We arrived in port without anything out of the ordinary happening.

I made one more trip with the same skipper to Gefle again. It was the last I was to make with him, as the owner had promoted him to another command of one of his best ships, a barque of 600 tons register, a regular trader to Quebec.

Our ship was given over to quite a different man to our late captain, who had been kind, considerate and thoughtful to the welfare of his men, for he could not give a command without a string of colourful adjectives. However, we had to put up with him. But he had to ship another crew as most of the present one refused to sail with him.

So we loaded up again and sailed for Wismar in Germany where we discharged and loaded again in much less time than at Gefle, and we set sail from there after being in port about three weeks.

When we reached Elsinore, a port on the coast of Denmark, the skipper went ashore and, as we were lying at anchor, he had to have the jolly boat and – of course – two of the crew. That meant that there were only four of us left, unless you include the mate's wife whom he was bringing home from Germany. With her, it made five hands all told and a very good fifth hand she made in the event, for she was a splendid sailor.

The captain had been ashore about four hours when a gale of wind sprang up: a regular fury of a breeze. As night came on it increased in intensity, so much so that we had to let go the second anchor, my word! You should have seen how that lady sailor worked, taking her place with the rest, pulling up the second cable and doing anything that a man could do. She told me all her people were sailors, women as well as men.

---

3   Sixpence, a "tanner", was worth 2.5p in decimal coinage, and threepence half that.

The gale lasted for two days and we thought the ship would drag her anchors and drift ashore, but she held on. It was so bad that the skipper was unable to get off to the ship, which delayed us three days. Then, with a fair wind blowing, when he did come aboard he started to curse and swear and blame the crew for his detention ashore, as if we could help it. The fact was he had no business to go ashore and he was thinking of the trouble there would be when he faced the owner.

We had rather a lively time on the rest of the passage home. I thought there would be a mutiny and no wonder, for the skipper was a perfect brute. How the men stood it I don't know. But as there were only a couple of days – all being well – before reaching port, I suppose they thought they would take no notice, but let him work his temper out.

It so happened there were two more vessels at Elsinore the same time as us. They did not stop, but signalled to the shore and sailed on, bound for West Hartlepool for different owners to ours. They got in port two days before us, whereas our vessel ought to have arrived first, being a much faster ship. You can imagine the surprise of our owner when we did arrive. He was walking up and down the quay, but he did not come aboard. Instead, he sent a message by one of the crew telling the skipper to come to the office as soon as the ship was made fast. What occurred when he did get there I do not know, but when he came aboard again he looked in a horrible temper. Speaking to no one, he went straight to his cabin and we saw no more of him that day.

The next morning, the owner sent one of his men from the shop to bring us two apprentices back with him. He had us both in his office separately to know what was the cause of the ship being delayed. How the skipper explained it, of course, we did not know and what explanation the other apprentice gave I knew nothing about, but when it came to my turn to explain, I told the owner the truth, for which I was to get it warm from the skipper a couple of days afterwards.

He went ashore again to see the owner. Now, whether my version of the ship's delay did not agree with his I do not know. But such was his temper when he came back that I believe he would have thrown me in the dock if he could have caught hold of me. However, I was a bit too quick for him.

He growled at me: "You wait a bit, you tailor-boy, 'till we get outside the harbour again. I'll take good care to see you won't have the chance to tell more tales to the owner concerning me!"

When we were loaded and hauled into the lock to go to sea, the tide serving our purpose some time after breakfast, all the crew and the other apprentice went ashore to have their morning meal as they all lived at Hartlepool. The skipper had his aboard.

So, while everybody was away, I packed up my belongings, slung my bag over my shoulder and stepped ashore. Nobody took any notice of me, which gave me an hour's start. I was outside the town and bound for Sunderland before the crew were due back from their breakfast.

2

I must go down to the seas again,
to the lonely sea and the sky,
And all I ask is a tall ship
And a star to steer her by.
— **John Masefield**

As luck would have it, I met up with a carrier's cart[1] going to the same place, so I had a lift all the way.

Getting into Sunderland, I made my way to the quay, but before boarding any ships, I went to a few public houses to try to get a few coppers as I was very hungry. I had had nothing to eat all day, having forgotten in my hurry to put a few ship's biscuits in my bag. I was not long in collecting enough money to get a good meal as well as the price of a night's lodging. The means by which I did this, you see, was because I happened to have a German concertina, which I played fairly well and which proved a little gold mine as I played dance tunes as well as songs.

After a good night's rest and a hearty breakfast, I made my way down to the docks, and after strolling along the quay looking for a likely ship I saw a brigantine, the captain of which was sitting on the rail aft smoking his pipe with his wife standing beside him.

"Good morning, captain. Have you shipped all your hands?" I inquired.

"No," he said. "I want a lad something like yourself. Are you in want of a berth?"

I told him that was indeed what I was looking for.

"Come aboard, then, and let me see what you are like and what you can do. Then, if you suit me, we will go up to the shipping office and I will sign you on."

---

1   Before the era of mass motor transport on motorways, goods were delivered by carriers, or cart-
ers, using horse-drawn vehicles. Even the smallest communities had a carrier, who would be a
vital and important personage in his area. For, as well as goods, he could usually be relied upon
for some tasty titbits of gossip, too.

His wife was standing by and she gave me a smile and went below with the skipper, to give him her opinion of me, I suppose.

So, having signed on, we went back aboard and I started work at once. The ship was already loaded and was only waiting to finish signing on her crew. I happened to be the last.

I found when I got aboard that the ship was what you might call a family one, the skipper being owner as well as master. He had no home ashore, but he and his wife lived aboard their ship. We all had our meals together, the skipper's wife acting as a sort of foster mother to us all. The ship was an exceedingly comfortable one. She had been a lightship in the Mersey and was as staunch and tight as it was possible to build a ship. She was called the *Anna* and was about 150 tons register.

We sailed on the evening tide of the same day bound for Plymouth. Next morning the skipper had me down in the cabin to go through a sort of cross-examination, his wife being there as well. I was not long in finding out the reason. It appeared that the skipper, though an excellent captain as far as the navigation of the ship was concerned, was a very poor scholar and he particularly wanted to know if I could – and would – keep his accounts for him. Of course, I had told him all about my schooldays and my reason for going to sea, although I left out the Hartlepool affair. I agreed to the skipper's request and his wife was very pleased that I was able to do what he required.

The captain was one of the very few who seemed to know the coast of Great Britain by heart. Should there be any signs of bad weather coming, or a sudden squall, he would simply say: "We must get in somewhere out of this." But where that "somewhere" was we had no idea, as it mostly appeared to the crew that we were running into some rocks, or onto a sandbank, until of a sudden we would find ourselves in a snug harbour to stay until the weather was a bit finer. On these occasions the skipper always took the wheel himself. Being the owner of the vessel, of course, he had no one to give account to as to delay or anything that happened during a voyage.

Having discharged at Plymouth, we left that port in ballast bound for Bowness up the Solway Firth to load coal for London. I never saw or handled coal like it before or since. It was called "cannel coal". It was hard as flint and very light – so light that we could not load the ship more than half her tonnage, though we had the decks loaded as well as the hold. It was also a very combustible coal. You could light it with a match. I almost caught the ship afire the first time I used it to light the galley fire, not having been told of its dangerous nature. It was consigned to a firm of aniline dye manufacturers.

From London we set sail for Poole to load pipe clay for Birkenhead and it was at Poole that I had to part company with the captain and his ship. Now, you must understand that the skipper was a Scotsman and did not like parting with any money if he could help it.

Chapter 2

It so happened just about when we got into Poole, it being the summer of 1866, that ree Trade Act[2] was passed by Parliament which meant – so far as the coasting trade was concerned – that vessels of any nationality could trade from port to port on any part of the British coast, which they very soon did. As they were unable to do so before the Act was passed, they took full advantage of it and the consequence was that freight fees became much lower and more difficult to get.

As I was not getting very much in the shape of wages – 30 shillings a month to be exact[3]– and having to work very hard, not including the keeping of the skipper's accounts, I asked the captain for a rise. He refused on account of the effects, he said, the Free Trade Act had started to have on his business.

"Very well, captain," says I. "If you won't give me any more money I must try for another ship. So will you please give me my discharge?"

This he also refused to do. My reply was to say: "If you won't pay me off, I must go to the shipping office and see what they say about it."

As he knew perfectly well that he could not refuse me in this matter, at least, he gave in and paid me off rather than pay me any more money in wages. I was sorry to have to leave the ship as I was very comfortable. My connection with the *Anna* ended with the captain and his wife wishing me "goodbye" as I stepped ashore, leaving the dinner half-cooked.

As there was no train leaving for London until the next morning, I strolled about having a look around. When it was time to think about something to eat, I went into a coffee shop to get it and who should be there but my late skipper and his wife having their tea ashore. They at once asked me to join them, but I could not very well do so under the circumstances, I felt. I sat at the next table instead.

I thought the skipper might want me to come back. This turned out to be the case, his wife telling me that I should not better myself elsewhere. I told them I would come back on board with them if the skipper would make my wages two pounds a month, but he would not give in. So I left them and went to look for lodgings.

---

2   A series of Free Trade Acts expanded commerce during the first half of the 19th century. By 1860, Britain was virtually a Free Trade country. The Act mentioned here was possibly one of 1866, which withdrew timber duty, making more competitive a trade the writer was to experience later. Ship owners were among the few objectors to the removal of protective tariffs for the reasons the writer gives. Young Thomas had a personal objection: it gave his canny Scots skipper the classic "business is bad" excuse for an employer to turn down a bid for a pay rise.

3   To put Tom's 30-shilling (£1.50) wage in context, a loaf of bread at this time would have been 6d (2.5p), with board and lodgings ashore 14 shillings (70p) a week (see Chapter 4). Bed and board were provided at sea, with life's little luxuries, such as clothes, soap and tobacco, sold to the crew by the captain from the ship's slop chest.

3

One road leads to London,
One road leads to Wales,
My road leads me seawards,
To the white dipping sails.
— John Masefield

Next morning I took the fast train to London and at once went to the docks to see what I could get in the shape of a berth, but I was not very successful. There were plenty of ships, but they were mostly for long voyages. I had thought of trying for a berth aboard one of them and made a few inquiries, but the money was very small and I wanted more – not less – than I had been getting.

Then I thought of Liverpool. So, still having a few shillings left, I went into Houndsditch and bought as much "jewellery" as I could afford with the little money I had to spare. My purchases consisted of brooches, tie-pins and the like.[1] As I had not had money enough for the rail fare, I had to tramp it. So, with a nearly new pair of sidespring boots which I had bought the day before starting, I faced the walk of 208 miles.[2]

It was the beginning of the month of August and beautiful weather. I was troubled very much with blisters on my feet on the first day, but they soon dried up and then I was able to walk like a professional. As I had no money for lodgings, I slept under the hedges. What little money I got from the sale of items in my stock of "jewellery" I had to keep for food.

When I got to Birmingham I picked up a chum: a clog-maker who was going to Liverpool to a job he had already got. So I had company.

---

1   Buying trade goods to barter along the way on a long journey, especially on foot, was partly for security. The footpad, or mugger of the day, would rather take cash than goods he would need to sell on and perhaps have to explain. Also, judicious haggling could talk up the value of trade items to get extra food or services in exchange.

2   Modern motorways must have cut some corners. A current road atlas of Great Britain gives the distance as only 195 miles.

There was plenty of fruit about, so I was able to get some by buying it with a bit of "jewellery". As we were passing a large orchard on the road we stopped and stood looking at a big apple tree, the branches of which were hanging over the road. Then the lady it belonged to came running out begging us not to touch the tree. She said she would give us plenty of other apples, which she did. Thus we were persuaded to spare her prize pippins, but we were still able to have a diet of juicy fruit for the next day.

When we got to Stafford I managed to trade to pay for a night's lodging and a good breakfast in the morning – the first square meal I had had since starting out from London, as I had only been able to afford bread washed down with water, which I had to drink by putting my mouth into the streams as I had no cup to drink out of.

When leaving Stafford we came upon an extraordinary scene. We had to pass the jail and outside were a great number of people. There was also a scaffold erected for an execution. All executions took place outside the jail in those days.[3] What impressed itself on me so much that I shall never forget it was the man, a young farmer about 30 years of age and finely built, who was brought out and placed on the scaffold for us all to see. On the bolt being drawn, the rope around his neck broke and then there was a scene, I can tell you. The man's friends tried to rescue him, but the police were too strong for them. In the meantime another rope had been got and the sentence duly carried out.

The prisoner looked ghastly on being put up a second time. There was a livid mark around his neck where the first rope had left its impression. I was very glad to get outside the town away from it all.

We then made our way to Crewe, where we stayed the night sleeping in a timber yard, then on to Warrington, having to sleep under a hedge that night, it being too far for Warrington to be reached. But we were up early and got there at about eight in the morning.

The weather was still beautifully fine and we sat down on a green bank and started to have our breakfast which consisted of bread and cheese we had obtained at Crewe. Opposite where we sat there were some large, red-brick buildings which turned out to be cotton factories. As we sat there, a number of girls came out of one of the factories, passing us as they went into another building close by. It appeared to be where they had their meals, for a few minutes after they had gone in two of them brought out a basin of tea for each of us saying it was "to swill down the bread and cheese". They then tarried beside us on our bank long enough for the four of us to enjoy a brief flirtation.

When I gave them a brooch each from my stock for their kindness, I found I had made a mistake as no sooner had the two girls gone back inside then out came about 20 more to see if they could get one each for themselves. I told them they were for sale, not to be given away. I was very sorry, for they seemed to think I was some kind of cheap-Jack with plenty of trinkets to give away. Nonetheless, it was very kind of their two

---

3   See Appendix C

sisters of mercy to give tea and a welcome taste of female company to two red-blooded lads on a fine summer's day.

My chum left me soon after as he said he wanted to visit a friend in Warrington before going on to Liverpool, so I went on to Birkenhead. I had not been there very long before I got a job aboard a barque. I took a stroll around the docks and almost the first vessel I came to was the *Anna* discharging her cargo of pipe clay. The skipper happened to be on deck. Seeing me, he invited me aboard and asked me if I had had any breakfast.

When I told him "No," he said: "Come on down below then and join us as we are just going to have ours." I thought this was very kind of him.

The first thing he wanted to know was whether I had got a ship.

"Yes, captain, but it is only for the run[4]," I told him. I had not expected to see him, or I should have boarded the *Anna* first.

Then he wanted to know why I spent so much money coming from London as there were plenty of ships to be got there.

"Yes," I said. "But not the one I wanted. They were mostly going on too long a voyage for my liking at present and besides, captain, I did not spend any money on a railway fare as I had not got it. I simply walked to Liverpool which took me four days and a half[5] – about the same time it took the *Anna* to get here."

I stayed aboard with him for the rest of the day, doing a little work putting some of his accounts straight to pay for his kindness, until it was time for me to get aboard the barque bound for Workington, at which port we arrived next day. I remained on board a few days to help dismantle her as she was going to lay up for repairs.

"Now," I thought to myself. "What shall I do? Stay here, or go to another port? As there did not seem any prospect of a ship in Workington, I decided on the latter course of action and tramped to Whitehaven where I knew there were regular traders to Newport in Wales carrying iron ore, so I decided to go there.

I had not enough money on me to pay my passage, so I asked the skipper of one of the steamships there if he would give me a passage. He did so on the understanding that I was to work for it. We had a terrible time of it as a gale sprang up soon after we left Whitehaven and continued the whole of the passage.

I had rather a shock the only night we were at sea. I could not sleep (I was lying on one of the lockers in the fo'castle) as the vessel was tumbling about so and I was getting quite sore. So I went on deck and, going aft, I found the man at the wheel almost asleep with the ship right out of her course. We were bound for Newport and the ship was heading for Douglas, Isle of Man.

---

4   For a single, one-way voyage only.

5   By Tom's own figures, this was 208 miles in four-and-a-half days – no mean feat, even for a fit youngster. He would have had to average 46 miles a day: at least 10 hours' brisk walking, not including stops on the way, such as to observe the public execution. Possibly he exaggerated a bit to impress his former employer with his robust physique and independent spirit.

Chapter 3

I gave the man a good shaking and asked him if he knew where he was steering for. He quickly put her on the right course and almost carried away the bridge in doing so as a very heavy sea dashed aboard through the helm being put up so suddenly.

That was the first time I had been on board a steamship at sea and, as far as my experience went, I made up my mind never to ship in one again, which resolution I kept the whole time I was at sea.

4

*West of these out to seas
colder than the Hebrides I must go, Where the fleet
of stars is anchored and the young
star captains glow.*

— **James Elroy Flecker**

Arriving at Newport, I made my way to a boarding house recommended to me by a man aboard the boat on which I came to the town. As I had very little money the boarding master, as he was called, agreed to board and lodge me for 14 shillings a week. He, of course, relied on my advance note for payment, as was the custom in those days. I was talking about 1866, to be precise. Whether it is so now I do not know, but I expect it is.[1]

Next morning I walked around the docks and the only ship that was signing on that day was an Irish barque hailing from Wexford. I met the skipper at the shipping office and made an arrangement with him before seeing the vessel, otherwise I do not think I should have shipped in her. She was a curious looking craft, being built like clipper for'ard and a Dutch galiot aft with her rudder-head about a foot above the taffrail. Otherwise she appeared to be all right.

---

1   Pity the poor – in more senses than one – matelot in parts of the world where this system of credit might still go on. The writer is describing a form of credit for seamen which was fair enough if treated with caution, as he was clearly canny enough to do.

However, it was universally abused in the system of "crimping". Boarding masters would meet ships as they docked, or before, and tout for custom among the sea-weary sailors. Credit for board and lodging, copious quantities of strong drink and more exotic creature comforts would be extended until Jack Tar wore out his welcome.

The "crimp" would then "sell" his client's labour to any skipper willing to advance wages to the tune of the often-inflated bill. The hapless seaman was then bundled aboard his new employer's vessel without having any say in the matter.

An unwary sailor could find himself trapped in a spiral of debt with advances of pay deducted to meet a crimp's bill leaving him so short at the end of his next voyage that he would have little alternative but to accept the blandishments of another crimp for credit.

As she was not sailing for a few days, I worked on board until the time of departure, having my meals at the boarding house as well as sleeping there. With loading completed and everything ready, we left Newport for Bermuda in the West Indies with a cargo of coal for the government.

When we got to sea I found our ship was not only strangely built, but also very slow and erratic in her sailing. You could not get any more than five knots out of her if it was blowing a gale, and if there should happen to be a head wind there was not the slightest chance of getting any nearer our destination. For she would go to leeward like a skate as though she were trying to sail broadside on.

However, we sighted Bermuda at last, but we had great difficulty in getting into the harbour. We had a pilot aboard and were just starting to shorten sail when one of those hurricanes for which Bermuda is famous caught us. It blew the ship on her beam ends, so that you could not stand on the deck, but had to hold on to the rigging, or anything you could get a grip on.

The pilot was on the topgallant fo'castle head swearing, cursing and tearing the wool on his head trying to let go the anchor. Meanwhile hundreds of people were on the quay without being able to render any assistance. It was no laughing matter, but if I had been going to the bottom the next minute I could not have helped but laugh at that pilot as I clung to the weather rigging.

Presently there was a loud report as if someone had fired a cannon. On looking we saw all the sails flying away in bits like a lot of birds and – incredible as it may seem – the wind blew every bit of canvas out of the bolt ropes. So there was nothing left but what looked like a lot of picture frames and one or two fore and aft sails that were reefed and stowed on their spars before the wind hit us. With that, the ship righted herself.

Now, all this lasted about five minutes. Another five minutes like that and we should have been sent to the bottom for sure. The curious part of the gale was that it came on without a moment's warning. The sky was quite clear and not a cloud to be seen. Also, there was no rain and after a few minutes all was the same as before, excepting the sails which the wind had so ruthlessly carried off. The skipper happened to be down below getting his papers ready when all this happened and there he had to stay until it was all over as the companionway door was jammed shut.

I was told when we got into dock that there was plenty of rain with some of these hurricanes which the local people depended upon for drinking as well as all other purposes. A person who owned plenty of water tanks in Bermuda was considered wealthy in the same way that someone in Great Britain in those days would be if he were a big landowner. I was also told that the quays around the docks were hollowed out into one huge tank owned by the government.

Walking along the beach outside the dock, I was surprised what a quantity of copper bolts and metal sheathing was lying about. There were tons of it I should think, showing what a number of wrecks must have taken place on – or near – the island. But no one was allowed to take any of the metal away. Why the government wished to keep it there was a mystery to me. But there – I suppose it was all later collected and turned into money.

We were in Bermuda about a month altogether, discharging our cargo and cleaning the ship up a bit. We had to bend a whole new suit of square sails, what they called the winter set. The sails we lost were old and very much patched. If we had had the winter set bent[2] when the hurricane struck us we should have gone to the bottom without a chance of any of us being rescued as every one of us was clinging to the rigging, or any thing we could hold on to. That was the closest I ever got to experiencing anything like being shipwrecked.

I was very glad to get away from Bermuda, for we were not allowed to go into Hamilton, the principal town, or about any other part of the island. Why that was I cannot imagine. It certainly was rather monotonous having to stay in the docks all the time with forts all around us.

So one fine morning we set sail for Savannah, Georgia, in the southern states of America. There we were to load pitch pine. The vessel, it appeared, was built for carrying as she had a large porthole cut into her starboard bow. It was about five feet square, so that she would be able to carry very large baulks of timber.

It took us about three days to get to Savannah, which we found was rather a difficult matter as the south of the river was blockaded. Ships loaded with stones had been sunk on both sides of the river leaving only a fairway for one vessel to pass through at a time, and not very large ones at that. If our ship had been two feet more abeam she would not have got through. The ships were sunk at the time of the Civil War to prevent blockade-runners from entering the port and there they had remained, though the war had been over for some 18 months.[3] As far as I could find out or see there were no docks at this port, all the quays and berths being built into the sides of the river. Most of the loading and discharging was carried out in mid-stream.

As we entered the river, which was early in the morning, we could see what kind of a paradise on earth we had come to. For there was a very heavy, yellow fog rising up from the land which is mostly marsh. Should any person happen to go ashore before the fog had cleared off, they would be very fortunate if they did not get the fever. The air is generally clear of the mist by about 11 in the morning, after which we saw the inhabitants getting out onto the rice plantations as all this marshland is given over to the growing of rice. This was the finest in the world I ever saw and was called "Carolina", this being the state on the other side of the river Savannah to Georgia.

---

2   The winter sails would have been of stouter canvas than their patched and thinner summer counterparts that blew out. They might have stood up to the violent winds, but, in so doing, caused the vessel to capsize.

3   The American Civil War ended on 9 April 1865. The prosperity of the writer's West Hartlepool employer (see Chapter 1 and Appendix B) as a result of providing meat for the Confederacy shows that Union blockading of Southern ports had limited success.

Having been piloted about a mile up the river, which is a very wide one, we had to let go both anchors as we were to stay there to load our cargo. I had often wondered how those very large baulks of timber were shipped. Well, this was the way of it. As soon as one of the stevedores came aboard, he had the jib boom unshipped and a very stout stay made fast to the foremast head and the other end to the head of the bowsprit. Then from the bowsprit head was fixed a very heavy chain sling with an iron block at the lower end through which a stout hemp rope was rove. This rope led down from the capstan on the fo'castle.

Then, after the ship's carpenter had opened the porthole, the work of loading commenced. After an iron roller had been fixed to the bottom of the porthole, a medium-sized baulk had a chain sling put round it. When all was ready a baulk was floated, stem on, to the porthole. The end of it was caught up by the rope I mentioned and the stevedores steered the end into the square space. Next, the rope was shifted further along the timber and was caught up by a hook which was fastened to the sling on the first-mentioned baulk. Every thing being ready, the crew heaved on the capstan and so raised the log of timber to the level of the porthole when it slid from its own momentum.

Thereafter men in the hold steered it into its place by means of rollers, but they could not get it right in, so the small log that was in the sling was brought into use as a sort of battering ram, a tackle being fastened at the aftermost part of the log worked by the crew aboard the ship. They pulled the log out as far as possible and then let go suddenly, the stevedores steering it straight to the porthole. About one good raise generally sent the log being loaded as far as required. I am not quite certain whether my description of the loading is correct in every detail, but as far as my memory goes, it is.

There was also a very strange – and very good – way they had of bringing the timber down to the port where it was to be shipped. The whole of our cargo was brought down the river some hundreds of miles from Savannah in one raft. What state, or states, it came from I do not know, but it took some weeks to arrive at the port of shipment. There were three huts built on the raft and a whole family lived in each hut, to say nothing of an enormous alligator which was lashed to the raft, frozen stiff. The raft was towed down the river by a very large tug with one big wheel at the stern to propel her. This tug was also a kind of warehouse with three floors all loaded with merchandise which had been collected en route.

It happened to be winter while we were at Savannah and it was fearfully cold. It is just the reverse in the summertime there, the heat then being unbearable.

I went through three plantations while we were there and they were all in a terrible state. What were once fine factories were now heaps of ruins with broken machinery all over the place. The emancipated slaves were having a very bad time of it with no work to do. They were half starved, living in old wooden shanties which they tried to keep warm with chips of wood from the river. As the river is infested with alligators, a large number of people lost their lives when collecting this wood.[4]

We were rather a long time in this port, the loading being a very slow affair. I think it was about five weeks before we started for Queenstown for orders.[5] When we got out into the Atlantic we found the weather much warmer. The reason for that was that we had got into the Gulf Stream and we had it with us for quite three parts of the passage.

We were about halfway across the Atlantic when we came across what appeared to be a derelict topsail schooner with both masts carried away and the sails for'ard hanging to the stays, but she was not damaged in any way. She looked like a smart vessel and seemed to have just had a fresh coat of paint. I think her cargo must have been fruit, for there was quite a nice smell coming from her. As we had none too much grub aboard our own vessel, the crew went aft to ask the skipper if they could lower a boat and row over to her to investigate whether or not there was anyone on board and perhaps obtain a supply of extra provisions or fruit. But the stubborn Irishman refused.

Then we suggested that we should take her in tow as salvage. This he also refused flatly, using a bit of flowery language in his refusal, but subsequent events made him sorry for his stubbornness. Why, we could have boarded her and been back in the course of an hour as we were quite close to her! There was very little wind and a lovely moon shining, the time being about eight bells in the first watch[6] [midnight].

I am sorry to say that we saw no more of the schooner as it came on to blow very hard during the night. Whether she sank or was blown away I could not say. Anyway, there was nothing to be seen of her from then on.

Now, it so happened that one of the crew was another Irishman named Murphy who was a native of the skipper's home town of Wexford. For some reason or another the pair of them were always quarrelling – what about, the rest of us could never find out. Then one morning we heard a squabble going on aft. Turning out to see what it was, we saw the skipper and Murphy having a set-to, going at it hammer and tongs. Murphy was evidently getting the worst of it as he was in a terrible mess, being covered in blood. As it was eight bells then [midday] and dinner time, he had to come for'ard. Then we washed him down. He was swearing all the time we were tending him and we thought he would turn in as it was his watch below.

He did nothing of the sort, but instead strode aft again, calling on the skipper to come up on deck and have another set-to. So up the skipper came.

---

4   In the winter of 1864, General William Tecumseh Sherman undertook his scorched earth march to the sea across Georgia. Ironically, the blacks freed in his wake apparently traded the tyranny of slavery for the no less cruel taskmaster of starvation as a result of their "liberator's" actions.

5   Merchant vessels reported to Queenstown (Cobh) County Cork, Ireland, or Falmouth in Cornwall "for orders" from their owners' agents as to which home port to go to for discharging their cargoes.

6   A system of four-hour working periods, or watches, divided the seaman's 24-hour day, with a pair of two-hour dog-watches in the afternoon. See glossary.

"Haven't you had enough?" he says to Murphy. "Ye want some more, do yez? Well, begorra, ye shall have it!"

So he picked Murphy up by the scruff of the neck and the seat of his trousers and threw him right amidships.

"Now perhaps ye'll be quiet. If ye don't, I'll pitch yez overboard," the skipper cries.

So Murphy lay still for a bit. I think he was stunned. Then he crawled into the fo'castle and turned in. He could not have been injured very much as he turned out all right next watch.

We were now nearing the Irish coast, expecting to make Queenstown in a couple of days or so, when the wind – which had been chopping about a lot – seemed to have set in from due east. To make matters worse, it came on to snow, blowing nearly a gale at the same time. So we had to shorten sail. Then we knew that if the wind kept in the same quarter we should be very lucky to get in anywhere!

As we were likely to be knocking about the coast of Ireland until the wind changed, the skipper bethought of the provisions and, on overhauling the pantry and bread locker, he found what he estimated to be about two days' stock.

So, as we were quite as likely to be out three or four weeks as so many days, we were cut down to two ounces of bread and one ounce of pork daily. The beef had run out some days before the skipper took stock. As a matter of fact, we were headed for three weeks and two days from the time the easterly wind started until we arrived at our destination.

I wonder what the skipper thought of the abandoned schooner now? He certainly had cause enough to regret not letting us scavenge for food aboard her when we had the chance. It was bad enough to have to put up with the weather, but when you had to be constantly on the go, watching every opportunity to make a little headway, making sail and taking it in again every few hours on an empty stomach, it made it doubly hard.

One day I was feeling very hungry, so I asked the skipper if he would let me sweep out the bread locker.

"Oh yes, me lad," says he. "But I don't think ye'll find much there."

Anyway, I got my tin plate and the cabin brush and swept up all I could, including cockroaches, maggots and weevils. I managed to get nearly a plateful of crumbs and creatures which I mixed up with some of the cook's fat, then I put it in the oven and baked it a lovely brown.

I had to keep watch over the galley while it was cooking or I should have lost it for sure to my starving shipmates. However, when it was cooked I took pity on them all and carried my makeshift baking into the fo'castle and shared it out with the watch who declared it was delicious. The cook had laughed when I took it to him to be baked, but when I removed it from his oven he cast very envious eyes over it.

Our cook was a darkie, and a regular Mark Tapley[7] – never so happy as when he faced misery. He used to try to keep our spirits up with his comical yarns and songs. He was also more than a little resourceful. He happened to have a small quantity of flour left in the barrel, so I suggested that he should make some bread with it.

"How can I do that without baking soda or yeast?" he asks.

"Well," I reply. "You can put a little flour in a pot and it will soon turn to yeast."

"Oh yes," he comes back at me. "But that would take a couple of days and we might be in port by that time."

So what did he do but get some common soda and tie it up in a piece of canvas, hanging it up inside the top of the galley funnel for a few hours. What little flour there was he made into bread in the shape of rolls. It was not all that bad as regards flavour, but there were a lot of yellow spots in it. Well, spots or no spots, we were very glad of it.

A few days after this luxury the wind took a turn for the better, veering round from due east to north-west after blowing from the east for nearly a month as a strong gale with plenty of snow and rain nearly the whole of the time. We were getting like a lot of scarecrows, so I was very thankful, I can tell you, when I came on deck one morning to find the ship rounding the Blaskets[8] with all sail set. It must have been hard work for the watch on deck to get everything "a' taut-o" as we were all weak as rats. I suppose it was the fair wind that bucked them up and made the work appear much easier than it really was.

So all being well and the wind continuing fair, we thought we should be off Queenstown in a couple of days, which we were. Having got the ship's orders regarding her destination, we squared the sails again – as we had not gone into the harbour proper – for Dublin.

The boat which brought off our sailing orders also brought us some provisions for which the skipper had signalled some time before reaching the harbour. While waiting for our orders we saw what was then an awesome sight: the *Great Eastern*[9] steamship making for Queenstown. My word, she did make a smother – a Newfoundland fog wasn't in it!

Mention of the *Great Eastern* puts me in mind of a yarn I was told by a shipmate at the time.

A Yankee vessel was going up the Thames when a boat came alongside her with all kinds of vegetables for sale. The greengrocer came on board with some cabbages.

---

7   Mark Tapley is Martin's invariably cheerful servant and companion in Charles Dickens's *Martin Chuzzlewit*. Whatever happens, Mark always believes things will "come out jolly".

8   Great Blasket Island is one of the westernmost rocky outcrops of Ireland, off the rugged coast of County Kerry's Dingle peninsula.

9   Isambard Kingdom Brunel's paddle steamer *Great Eastern* was built by Scott Russell at Milwall, London, and launched in 1858; she was the largest vessel afloat at the time. She was 691 feet long with a beam of 83 feet and of 22,800 tons register. Used for some years for cable-laying in the Atlantic and Mediterranean, she ended her days in 1888, when she was sold to be broken up.

Isambard Kingdom Brunel's Great Eastern
(courtesy of National Maritime Museum, Greenwich, London)

"Do you call them cabbages?" declares the steward. "Why, we grow cabbages as big as *that*," pointing to the dome of St Paul's Cathedral which was visible in the distance.

The greengrocer said nothing for a moment or two. Then they were passing the shipyard where the *Great Eastern* was being built.

"What is that darned thing they're building?" inquires the steward.

"Oh that," retorts the greengrocer. "It's only a pot they are making to boil your Yankee cabbages in!"

Having arrived at Dublin and made the ship fast, the whole of the crew went ashore to the first restaurant we could find and had a good meal washed down with the finest stout I ever drank. The next day after our arrival we went up to the shipping office to get paid off. The skipper kindly crossed out our tobacco accounts[10] to make up for us being half-starved.

---

10 Ships carried stores of spare clothing, personal equipment and some luxuries, such as tobacco, which were sold on credit to members of the crew by the captain. The store was called the "slop chest". The cost of the slop chest goods, plus a small profit for the skipper cum seaborne shopkeeper, were recovered from seamen's pay at the end of a voyage when they signed off.

5

No private views disgraced our generous zeal,
What urged our travels was our country's weal;
And none will doubt but that our emigration
Has proved most useful to the British nation.

— George Barrington

Then I went to London, crossing over from Dublin to Holyhead in the cattle boat which also carried passengers. This was in early 1867 when I was 21 and came of age. Among the passengers were a great number of emigrants bound for the United States, who all had to stay on deck during the passage. All the luggage each had was done up in a bundle in a handkerchief.

As we were going down the River Liffey the emigrants were having a fine old time singing and dancing, until we neared the mouth of the river where the water got a bit choppy. Then we saw a great change in their antics. One by one they fell on the deck being overcome by seasickness. I could not help laughing when one went to sympathise with another, offering him a drop out of a bottle of strong drink then toppling over himself, being very sick at the same time from the twofold effects of the liquor and the motion of the ship. Before we had been outside in open water an hour I think the whole lot of them were lying on the deck one on top of the other, sick and groaning. It was not a pretty spectacle to behold.

Having reached London and wanting to get to Newport, Wales, I had a look round the docks, finally picking a ship going there in ballast.

She was called the *Battersby*, London being her port of registry. She was an old East Indiaman[1] and about 1000 tons register. I thought I could save some money and earn

---

1   East Indiamen were vessels that were veterans of the East India Company's lucrative trade with the Far East. They were built of the best materials, largely to withstand the extreme conditions of a tropical climate, where giant and voracious woodworms could eat their way through a hull, given time. The designs of East Indiamen, usually vessels of some 1300 tons, were considered old-fashioned but style was not necessarily a priority to cost-conscious ship owners and masters.

some at the same time by signing on with her, for the rail fare from London to Newport was more than my pocket would stand. So I went aboard and interviewed the skipper who appeared to be a very pleasant man. He was quite willing to ship me for the run to Newport, though he said he would rather I signed on for the round voyage. Once he had put this proposition to me – with Newport on the itinerary – I told him I was content to sign on there and then as it would save me a lot of trouble as well as boarding house money.

So having come to terms, I went ashore to get a fresh kit. My clothes I carried about with me, also my blanket, but the mattress I always threw overboard on nearing port.

Next morning I went to the shipping office with the skipper and signed on. Then, having got my advance note, I went and made a few more purchases after getting the note cashed in a pub, for which accommodation I had to pay two shillings and sixpence.

As the ship had not quite loaded her ballast and most of the "runners" had to be shipped, we were likely to be a week before sailing. A runner is a man who does not take long voyages, but only ships in vessels that are going to another port around the coast to load for foreign parts. The runner then trusts to get another ship for his run back home.

I went aboard at once and started work. I happened to be cooking as the cook had not shipped aboard yet. So I saved a week's board and lodging. As I was a fairly good hand at getting the meals, the skipper suggested that I should take on the cook's job, but I told him I did not care for it, preferring to be an able seaman.

During the time I was aboard before leaving the docks I was able to see the kind of accommodation the East India Company gave the masters of their ships in those days. Well, the cabin was the finest I ever saw, being made of mahogany and rosewood beautifully carved and polished. The bunks, or sleeping berths, were made of the same. All the brasswork that was needed – and there was plenty of it – was of beautiful design. I will not attempt to describe it as there was so much. What the steward thought of it I should not like to say as he had to do all the polishing.

It was about eight days after my going aboard that we set sail for Newport to load for Quebec. When we were loaded and out to sea I found she was a very good seagoing ship. It was very rarely that we shipped any water and then only when the weather was at its roughest. She had extremely high bulwarks about six feet from the decks, so when you had to go aloft you had to do a bit of climbing before you started.

We were about four weeks on the passage as the ship was rather slow. It would take half a gale of wind to drive her at six knots. Just as we got to the south of the St Lawrence River a very heavy fog came on, so we had to shorten sail, which delayed us a bit. When we were entering the river the fog being thicker than ever, looking almost like a blank wall, and we saw something very strange: the topgallant sails of a ship coming down the river, but no ship. It was just as if someone had stuck them on top of the fog. We crawled on until we were in sight of her and the distance between us was no more than the ship's length. If this had happened at night one – or both – vessels would have been lost. You could keep on blowing the fog horn, but the fog being so dense, the sound could not penetrate it. The ships got close enough for the two skippers to congratulate each other on their lucky escape.

Having arrived at Bic – pronounced "beak" – the port where you had to pick up your pilot for Quebec, we dropped anchor, the skipper saying that we should stay there for a few days and get some fresh provisions.

Now, I don't know if any readers of this book have been up the St Lawrence River, but if they have, they will have noticed that it is dotted over with some small islands, and it was to one of these that four of us took a trip in the jolly boat on a fine Sunday morning as we were given to understand that a lot of wild fruit grew on them. So, having landed on one of them, making the boat fast to a tree, we started to investigate to see what we could find.

Sure enough, there was fruit a-plenty. Gooseberries were thick on their bushes and an abundance of little shrubs about one foot high were covered with cranberries and whinberries. How the fruit got there is a mystery, but there it was, and we filled all the buckets we had brought with us with fruit (we had no baskets) and took them on board, giving them to the cook to bake the crew some pies, the skipper allowing him extra flour to make them with. My word! It seemed we were going to live quite luxuriously.

While we were staying at Bic, the captain went ashore and bought a live bullock from a farmer at sixpence a pound as it stood in the field – the farmer to kill it and dress it for its hide and offal. After it was killed and cut up, it was brought aboard, the best joints being slightly salted and hung up from one of the fore and aft stays to dry in the sun for cutting off steaks as they were required. The remainder was put into harness casks for keeping, so sometimes we had steak for dinner; at others we had meat puddings, always with plenty of vegetables. As I said, it appeared we were going to live a bit – and we did!

The cook, therefore, had a good deal to do while we were living at Bic. He would commandeer any of the crew who were about at any time when he wanted someone to assist him, which we very willingly did, I can assure you.

What a difference there was in the commanders of different ships! In the case of this vessel there was not a man aboard that would not do anything for our skipper, and they were a mixed crowd, I can tell you.

Well, we were lying there about a week when the pilot came aboard and we upped anchor and sailed for Quebec. I did not go ashore very often while we were there as it was rather a rough place to get about, especially at night, so I cannot say much about it. I was quite comfortable enough aboard without rambling about ashore.

Ours being rather a large vessel, she took us a long time to load. It was nearly a month before we finished loading, having to wait days sometimes for parcels of our cargo. This was all 14- or 16-foot deals, a deal being a British measure for timber planks nine inches wide, not more that three inches thick and at least six feet long. I should mention that the cargo was all shipped and stowed by the crew, men on shore simply putting one of the deals on the rail of the ship. What would seamen of today think of that?

At last we were loaded and set sail bound back to London. Having arrived off Bic again, the skipper went ashore and repeated his purchase of a bullock and had it pickled as before, also buying as many vegetables as he thought would keep: mostly swede turnips and potatoes. Then, having dropped the pilot, we started again for London. I am pleased to say we were not troubled with any fog on getting to sea, although there were a few icebergs knocking about which we managed to steer clear of.

We had been out a few days with a fine north-west wind blowing almost to a gale when a very curious thing happened. It was on the night of the fifth day out; the wind – still blowing from the same direction – started to gust a bit stronger, and as it did so the whole of the ship was suddenly lit up. Every yard arm end, the jib boom end and mast heads were lit up with a blueish white flame about one foot high. What was the cause of it we did not know at the time, but the skipper said it must be electricity in the air.[2] That certainly appeared to be so.

Still, there was nothing seemingly to cause the air to be overcharged with electricity, for it was a very fine night with the stars shining brilliantly, but the next day we had something that might explain things a bit. For although the wind kept in the same direction, it started to rain heavily, with plenty of lightning and thunder. The gale was so strong that it carried away our foretopsail. So all hands had to turn to and bend another, the watch from below having to do so in their drawers and singlets in the face of the emergency.

The lights that so brightly lit up our ship were similar to what we called "Jack o' Lanterns",[3] seen sometimes rising up out of boggy or marshy land. I went aloft and brushed my arm over two or three of them, but they all shone up again. It was certainly a very curious spectacle. What a boon it would be if the Clerk of the Weather would arrange it so as to have all ships so illuminated on approaching our foggy latitudes!

After these strange happenings, we had fine weather all the rest of the passage home, duly arriving in London. We dropped anchor in the River Thames where the ship was to discharge her cargo into barges. I did not stay in London, but went to Newport to my old boarding house, to have a few days' holiday before shipping again.

---

2   This not uncommon phenomenon is called St Elmo's Fire. It is caused by electrical discharges from ships' spars exposed to intense electrical fields in thundery conditions at sea.

3   A will o' the wisp. See glossary.

6

His flight was madness; when our actions do not,
Our fears do make us traitors.

— **William Shakespeare**

I liked my trip to Quebec so much I that thought I would make another voyage there if I could find a ship bound for that port. So it was, while walking along the quay, I saw a full-rigged ship very similar to the barque I was lately in. I inquired as to where she was bound and was told she was sailing for Quebec in two days' time.

I waited about with my discharges in my pocket to see the skipper. As he came on deck I asked if he had shipped all his crew. He said he had not, so I offered my services.

"Have you got your discharges with you?" he inquires.

"Oh yes," says I.

So I showed them to him and he seemed quite satisfied and told me to be at the shipping office next morning at 10 and he would sign me on with the rest of the crew.

Then, everything being ready, we set sail for Quebec. This was in the summer of 1867, as I recall. This was a very uneventful voyage with nothing much happening worth recording. We simply arrived at Quebec, discharged and loaded again with timber bound for Sharpness, where our cargo had to be discharged for a Gloucester firm.

After being paid off, I made my way back to Newport to my old boarding house, which by this time had got to be quite like a home to me. I asked the boarding master if there was anything in the dock signing on crew.

"Not much," he says. "But if you want a short trip, there is a little brig about two hundred tons signing on sometime this week bound for Naples."

He told me what part of the dock she was lying, so I went and had a look at her. She seemed a likely looking craft as she lay under the loading tip. I went aboard and, seeing the mate, asked him if the skipper had got all the hands he needed.

"No, I don't think so," says he. "There have been several aboard, but whether they have agreed to sign on I don't know, but I'll ask the skipper for you."

Down below he went and was up again in a few minutes saying that only two had agreed to be at the shipping office when she was signing on.

"I suppose you've got your last discharge with you?" he asks me. "If so, you had better see the skipper now. He'll be on deck in a few minutes."

Sure enough, when he came up I asked him if he had got all the men he wanted.

"No," he says. "I want two more." So after looking at my discharge he told me to be at the shipping office next morning to sign on. Though the ship looked quite smart lying in the dock, she was very different when at sea as we were to find out to our cost.

The crew being all aboard, also the pilot, we set sail for Naples. We had not been in the Bristol Channel an hour before it came on to blow and before we got to Lundy Island it was roaring a regular gale. Such roaring westerlies mark any sailor's September in the Western Approaches. We could see that the ship was not going to weather it. The seas were fairly smothering her, so the skipper decided to run back.

We dropped the anchor in Penarth Roads and all the crew went below. There we found everything to be afloat. There wasn't a dry spot to be found in the fo'castle. The water had been coming in through the deck, which we found to be like a sieve. We hadn't even a dry spot to sit down on. So when we had had our tea – which we had to have on deck – we had a confab. One of our number said he was going to swim ashore as he was determined not to go any further in a ship like that. We did not say anything to the skipper as we knew that would not mend matters.

We had not been anchored more than a couple of hours when a schooner – also running back – dropped her anchor ahead of us and came right athwart our hawser, grinding her side on our cable and cutting a great gash in her port side. After a lot of trouble she was got off and we helped the crew of the schooner to nail some tarpaulins over the damaged side. In the meantime she had taken in a lot of water and the pumps had to be kept going continuously.

As it was the ebb tide, they could not get into the dock so had to wait until the tide turned, keeping the pumps going all the time. The schooner had not only damaged herself, but also had done considerable damage to our ship, carrying away our jib boom and knocking the head of the bowsprit to pieces.

Now, all this happened the first day we were out, and as the skipper said he was not going into dock, but would have the carpenters off to repair the damage while the vessel lay in the roads, we decided what to do. There were four of us in the fo'castle, that being all the ABs she carried, with the mate, cook and steward sleeping aft.

When the skipper had been long enough below to be – as we thought – asleep, as well as the others, we made up our minds on our plan of action. We got all our duds up and put them in the jolly boat, which was slung up in the davits on the port quarter. Then, having fastened the companionway door so as not to be disturbed by those below, we put a coil of rattling line in the boat and got her outside the rails, lowering her down as quietly as possible. Then, every thing being ready, we unhitched the tackles, leaving them hanging over the side, and made for Penarth.

As I was pretty well-acquainted with the beach thereabouts, I took the tiller and steered the jolly boat to the most likely landing place where there were a few trees pretty close to the beach. So once we were ashore we took the coil of rattling line which had been fastened to the boat before we started and secured it firmly to a tree. This we did as we had no wish to get into trouble for losing the boat as well as deserting the ship, should we be apprehended.

The weather had cleared up and a bright moon was shining, so we tramped along until we came to a large farm where there were several big haystacks. Settling under the lee of one of them, we made ourselves comfortable for the rest of the night, it being about two o'clock when we left the ship.

As soon as we were awake we made our way further into the outskirts of Penarth as we wanted to keep close until nightfall, for there was sure to be a hue and cry after us. After tramping across some fields we came to a cowshed, or something of the kind, and as there did not seem to be any cattle about we went inside and made ourselves as comfortable as we could. As by this time we were getting hungry, I volunteered to go into the village to get something to eat. I procured a couple of loaves and some cheese to appease our appetites. We got plenty to drink from the streams that were gushing out of the ground just outside the shed where we had sought shelter.

The evening came on and it began to get dark. We started to tramp to Swansea as we had agreed to do while in the shed, but we had not gone many yards before one of our party decided he wanted to go to Cardiff to see an uncle who he said would most likely give him some money and a good supper to all of us. I'm sorry to say uncle did nothing of the sort. For after hearing his nephew's yarn, he turned us away from the door telling us to go to a boarding house as he did not want to be troubled by the police.

So we went to a well-known sailors' "home from home" and asked the housekeeper if he would put us up. He agreed to do this on the advance note system, he thinking that we had been paid off that morning and little guessing we were deserters as we each had our kit bags with us. We had been in the house about an hour having a bit of a rest and a smoke when we were told to go to bed. We had just got into bed when we heard some heavy tramping up the stairs. We thought it was the police, but it was the landlord in a deuce of a temper and swearing like a well-seasoned salt.

"Come out of there, you damned liars!" he cries. "Just been paid off, have you? I believe you are the crew that deserted your ship yesterday and I've a good mind to hand you over to the police. Get out of it quick before I change my mind."

So out we came without arguing the point, but we almost choked with laughter when we got a few yards away. As we had to be very much on the alert we kept our eyes

The Bute Street Bridge, Cardiff – where the fugitive, Tom Sullivan,
stopped for a smoke – still stands today

peeled, for the police would be sure to be on the lookout for men with their bags on their shoulders.

When we came to the bridge in Bute Street I thought I would go into the shadows there and have a smoke. So dropping my bag on the pavement, I sat down on it to enjoy a cigarette. Luckily for me my bag was black in colour, and as the other chaps did not know exactly where I had gone they could not give any information to the policeman who I watched arrest them while I was having my smoke break.

I sat there for a bit to let the policeman and his prisoners get well on their way to the police station, then I got up and went looking for a pawn shop which I very soon found. In I went with my bag to see what sort of a bargain I could make with "Moses" or "Isaac" as the case may be, for they were all Jews in the pawnbroking trade.

"Vell, vot can I do for you, my son?" says he as he looked at my bag.

"I'm hard up, Mo, and I want to know what you'll give me for this bag of clothes, bag and all."

So I turned the things out, among which there was a brand new pilot suit, the rest of the contents being in very good order too.

"Well, Ikey, what'll you give me for the lot?" I asks.

After he had looked it all over he offered me a paltry 14 shillings. You see, he had heard of the missing – or should I say runaway? – crew and made his offer accordingly.

"Make it twenty shillings and you shall have it," I says.

"You must be quick," he hisses, eyes popping out of his head to emphasise the urgency, "or the police will be here."

"Well, Ikey," says I, unmoved by his histrionics, "I would rather go with them than be cheated by you. But, look here, I'll make a bargain with you. If you'll let me have a shore-going suit – second-hand will do – and the money, you can take the lot and even then you will get about four times the value of what you are giving."

So, after a lot more haggling and hand-wringing, he agreed. Then we went into the back room where he fitted me out, cap and all, and it was an ordinary-looking individual that came out of the shop, whatever sort of "admiral" had gone in!

As soon as I was out of the pawnbroker's I made my way to the nearest coffee shop and secured a bed for the night. I turned out in the morning – which happened to be a Sunday – pretty early and strolled to the railway station to see how the trains served. I made inquiries and found that the train was due in about 15 minutes' time, so I went across to the inn opposite to have a little refreshment and a smoke after my long walk. I found there was an early train leaving Whitchurch, a short distance from Cardiff, for Bristol, and I thought that would be better than running the risk of going from Cardiff itself.

Going back to the coffee shop, I had a good breakfast before walking to Whitchurch. The licensed houses adjacent to the station were opened for business half an hour before the trains were due in those days.

Presently the train arrived and I started for Bristol, a place I had never been to before. The proprietor of the inn at Whitchurch had recommended a landlady to me, who lived at a part called Jacob's Well close to the docks. There I made my way from the station when I arrived. I explained to the landlady that I had not much money, but would give her my advance note as soon as I obtained a birth. As I gave her the money for my first night there, she said everything would be all right, but I'm sorry to say that a few years later I found her anything but all right.[1]

---

1   Here we are introduced to the mysterious Bristol landlady, in whom Tom, alias Jack, appeared to place some trust, even with his hard-earned wages. It is not beyond the realms of possibility that he had hopes of their relationship developing, but this was not to be, as it turned out.
Meanwhile, it seems that Jack probably felt it wise to lie low for a while lest he be caught and imprisoned for both deserting his ship and "stealing" the jolly boat, not to mention being party to locking the officers in their quarters. The penalties at the time for such a combination would undoubtedly have been severe. Even 50 years after the event, he might have thought it discreet to ignore this period. At any event, the next chapter of his story refers to a voyage that he took two years later.

$$7$$

I must have the gentleman to haul and draw with the mariner and the mariner with the gentleman. I would know him that would refuse to set his hand to a rope, but I know there is not any such here.

— **Sir Francis Drake**

Some two years later when I had reached 23 years of age I was lodged in Bristol again. There I looked for a berth and found a ship, the *Margaret Ann*. She was a full-rigged vessel and had just finished discharging, lying in Cumberland Basin ready to leave by the next tide for Cardiff to load for Martinique, a French island in the West Indies.

The *Margaret Ann* was a 718-ton barque built in St John's, Newfoundland, in 1851. Owned by Rawle and Company, she was 138 feet long with a beam of 28 feet. I went on board and saw the skipper, Captain Henry Nicholas, who was rather elderly, being 70 years of age, but quite a gentleman. After a bit of a palaver, he agreed to ship me there and then on 7 August 1869, first as a "runner" and then, when he shipped the full crew at Cardiff, as one of their number.

I was rather glad, for the ship was another East Indiaman about the same tonnage as one I had sailed in before, so I knew she would be a comfortable ship and not in too much of a hurry: "more days, more dollars", you know!

So after shipping 2000 tons of coal we set sail for St Peter's, Martinique, and in due course arrived in port. The island was a lovely place and, ours being a large vessel, we had a long stay there. In fact, it was much longer than we were entitled to.

It was this way. Our ship had four weeks' laying days: that is, the number of days in which her cargo has to be discharged. Now, it so happened that a number of smaller vessels continued to arrive for the same firm and so the discharging of our ship was delayed time after time until her time was up. This meant great expense to the firm as the expenses were doubled every day she was delayed over her time. This was what they called "demurrage".

Bristol's Cumberland Basin. The lock in to the River Avon can be clearly seen
(courtesy of National Maritime Museum, Greenwich, London)

Then one fine morning we heard a great rumpus on shore and looking over the side we saw the stevedore had arrived with all his "ladies" to start on the cargo. I should think there were over 200 of them. There were only about six men and they started to take off all three hatches as they were going to work them all at the same time.

My word! Talk about hustling. The hatches were no sooner off than they started on the cargo. The women brought their baskets to be filled then carried them on their heads down a plank to the quay. The baskets were made of chip and shaped like half a lemon. They held about half a hundredweight.

The men filled the baskets and the women lined up in a queue taking their turns. Some of them at the end of the queue danced and sang while they waited.

As soon as the coal got low enough in the hold the crew had to go below and fill larger baskets and hoist them on deck. It was a strange sight and it sounds very primitive, but they carried our 2000 tons of coal on to the shore in less than a week in those little baskets. I never saw work carried out like it in my life. It was nothing but a great heap of good humour, if I may use such an expression. The women were dancing and cracking jokes, I suppose, from the way they laughed at each other. I believe the firm was going to give them some kind of a reward if they cleared the ship in less than a week, which they did.

I mentioned earlier what a beautiful place Martinique was. The scenery was lovely and the mountains which cover a good part of the island were covered with various plantations, mostly sugar and coffee. The lowest parts were planted with different kinds of vegetables and fruits.

Chapter 7

The outside sanitary arrangements were quite in keeping with the rest. The streets were all paved with neat cobblestones and trees were planted each side of the thoroughfare. A clear stream of water running down from the mountains kept the roads quite cool as it ran down a rather deep gutter. The place was a regular paradise, so much so that I had an idea of deserting ship again to stay there!

However, discretion prevailed and I set my mind to the next leg of our voyage which meant that we now had to sail to Quebec again to load heavy timber for Bristol. It took us some time to reach there, our vessel being very much on the slow side. As soon as we arrived off Bic we shipped the pilot and continued our voyage, arriving at Quebec the next day. As they were expecting us, the shippers had got everything ready, so having got the gear fixed we were able to start loading at once.

Now among the crew was a half-breed American Indian, or something of the sort, with a complexion of a pale copper colour. He was a fine-built fellow and was over six feet in height with strength accordingly. He was also a very good seaman, but very taciturn, never having much to say. So far, so good. But the man was a perfect fiend when he had had a few glasses of whisky, or whatever they call the vile stuff that was generally sold as liquor in Quebec. One evening after we had knocked off, the half-breed and a young man hailing from Guernsey went ashore together. Where they went or what they were doing while there we didn't know, of course, and they had not come back aboard by the time the crew turned in for the night.

It was about eight bells in the first watch [midnight] when we heard a tremendous racket on deck. On turning out of the fo'castle to see what it was all about, we saw the half-breed holding the Guernsey chap up in the air and then throwing him down onto the deck. The pair of them were mad drunk. We managed to part them and get them in their bunks without the captain being disturbed.

Quebec in the 19th century (courtesy of National Maritime Museum, Greenwich, London)

The next morning as we were having breakfast the half-breed sat down on a chest in front of the Guernseyman's bunk, the latter having not turned out yet. All at once the half-breed jumped up and pulled the other fellow out of his bunk and started to pummel him. Then we grabbed him and hustled him out on deck where one of the crew lassoed him and made him fast to the foremast, the police flag being hoisted meanwhile.[1] In a very few minutes the police boat came alongside and, having handcuffed the half-breed, took him off to lock him up. He said not a word during the whole time this was going on. Next day he was had up before the magistrates and I believe got three months in clink, so the skipper had to ship someone in his place.

We finished loading without any further mishaps and set sail for Bristol. On getting out to sea I noticed – the same as I had on the passage out – that the ship was very hard to keep on her course, giving the man at the helm plenty to do by whirling the wheel about. She was a vessel that yawed about a lot, which made you think she was going off her course when she was doing nothing of the kind. So one night when it was my two hours at the wheel I happened to look over the stern and saw that her wake was as straight as a line, so I turns round and steers her by the wake! Then, instead of twirling the wheel round and round, I could steer her by a couple of spokes, taking a glance at the compass now and again.

After being about three months on the round voyage we duly arrived in Bristol and I was paid off on 24 November 1869. I made my way to Jacob's Well to see if everything was all right regarding my advance note. The landlady did not offer me any change I noticed, but she was very glad to have me back. So I stayed ashore for a bit, having a look around to see what sort of a place Bristol was. I much preferred the town as it was then to what it is now.

"Jack," says my landlady one day.

"Yes, ma'am."

" Do you know that a fine-looking schooner is signing on this week?"

"No," says I, "I do not as I have not been to the shipping office yet since I came home."

"Oh, I thought you might like to try to ship in her."

You see, I was getting rather slack in my payments and she thought it was time I made a move.

"All right, missus," I says. "I'll have a run down to the docks and see what this vessel of yours looks like."[2]

---

1   This must have been some local arrangement as there is no recognised flag signal specifically for summoning police to a vessel. The international code flag V ("I require assistance") might have been used, but might only have served to confuse those seeing it in a harbour.

2   The fact that this homely little exchange would seem to have stuck in Jack's memory all those years is another hint as to his relationship with his landlady tending more to the domestic rather than merely being a business arrangement. Maybe this was wishful thinking on his part, since the lady clearly had an eye to getting her rent in cash rather than kind.

8

Have you news of my boy, Jack?
Not this tide.
When d'you think that he'll come back?
Not with this wind blowing and this tide.

— Rudyard Kipling

She was a very smart topsail schooner, the *Estephania*, one of the prettiest vessels for a trading craft I had ever seen. I learned that she was built as a yacht for a gentleman on the east coast, but something went wrong with his banking account, so she was sold and put into the Newfoundland fish trade. Her registered tonnage was only 114 tons. At that time it was only small vessels that traded in the fish line. She was built by Harvey's, of Ipswich, in 1859 for a Mr Hootens. Her length was 93 feet and her beam 20 feet.

I had no difficulty in getting shipped. I was the only able seaman she carried. The rest of the crew was made up of an ordinary seaman (who was also cook), boatswain, mate and the skipper who did his share of the work as well as the rest of us, and we all had our meals together in the cabin aft. In fact it was quite a family ship, like a Dutch galiot.

We were to load coal and Champagne for a big merchant in St John's, Newfoundland, and it did not take long to get the cargo aboard. She only wanted the wine which was on its way from France, and as it duly arrived on the day we signed on we set sail without delay.[1] It was transhipped from one vessel to the other, which saved expense.

Then we set sail three days before Christmas. My word! What a time we were destined to have. For we had got as far as latitude 55, longitude 10 (off the west coast of Ireland), when a gale started to blow from the north-west and increased in violence as time went on. So bad was it that we never made but a couple of miles on our voyage

---

1   14 December 1869, according to Tom Sullivan's certificate of discharge.

for three weeks. Then the ship began to make bad weather of it and we were forced to put out a floating anchor. That is, some spars were lashed together and the spare anchor lashed to the spars then put over the weather rail to keep the ship's head to windward and head-on to the seas.

So with only the fore staysail set and the helm hard over the ship behaved so much better that all the crew (excepting the man at the wheel who had to keep a lookout as well) were able to stay below the same as the anchor watch. We stopped shipping any seas and were only troubled by the heavy spray as the seas dashed against the bows, but we took no notice of that. I believe that floating anchor was the salvation of the ship.

However, as we ought to have been in St John's by that time (just over three weeks out) we ran short of provisions, so the mate proposed that we run down to the Western Isles (the Azores) to procure some. The skipper was rather loth to accede to the proposal, but we had to have something to eat and we only had about three days' supply aboard. So after a little thinking he said he would try it as it was quite a fair wind to the south. What he was afraid of was that the ship might broach to under the operation and get swamped, the seas being so heavy.

Then he sang out to the boatswain to get the cable on to the windlass and haul in the floating anchor. The skipper took the wheel, watching all the time for an opportunity to bring her round between seas. So having got the anchor aboard she commenced to fall off and got on to her southern course without any mishap, which was wonderful considering the heavy seas. The topsail being set close-reefed during these operations, the vessel took her new course beautifully, rising and falling with the seas like a gull.

We soon got out of the limits of the gale and in a couple of days sighted Terceira in the Azores, where we lay off to communicate with the shore. After a while a boat came off and passed a note to the skipper by a long stick with a cleft end. None of the boat's crew would come aboard, the inhabitants there being afraid of contagion. So the skipper had to make his wants known in writing. I suppose there must have been somebody at the consulate who could read English. How we should have liked a run ashore!

They did not keep us waiting long before they came off with the provisions as well as some fruit in the shape of oranges, grapes and bananas, all of which – I believe – the skipper had ordered. He being half-owner, he was at liberty to do as he pleased.

So having obtained a good supply of provisions our skipper thought it advisable to make our course straight for the West Indies as we should be more likely to make our port in less time as well as being more comfortable than steering direct to St John's. We then made our course straight for Bermuda which we sighted in about eight days after leaving Terceira. Then we headed for Newfoundland. All went well until we got in the latitude of Cape Cod. Then we ran into some more weather, it being bitterly cold with a lot of ice about, though the wind was favourable.[2]

---

2   It seems the skipper took a calculated risk in setting out from Bristol to take the northern Great Circle route to Newfoundland. However, the storm off Ireland saw to it the gamble did not pay off. Having lost so much time and – as part-owner of the vessel – without anyone clamouring for

What made the working of the vessel much harder was the spray as it came aboard and immediately froze, so we were ankle deep in crushed ice, to say nothing of the running gear being frozen up. However, we reached our port at last. But having sighted the harbour, the thing then was how were we to get in? It seemed the pilot had had the same thought as ourselves, for he brought off half a dozen men with cudgels to beat down the sails which were thick with ice, the rigging being the same. Every rope's end was as big round as a man's wrist. At the same time that the pilot and his men were getting the ice out of the rigging and sails a tugboat was sweeping the harbour mouth free of floes of ice. So everything being clear, we got into the docks without any mishap.

There were no other vessels in the dock then. We discharged our coal and champagne[3], then loaded fish for Pernambuco, Brazil. Just as we started loading, another schooner arrived in ballast to load fish for the same port. There was a very great difference in the care and manner of shipping fish to Brazil and that shipped to some home port, all the fish being packed as to quality and size then packed into round drums with a maple leaf between every fish, each drum holding about 56 pounds. The merchant was on the quay every day while loading was going on. He would have come down the hold to see to the stowing, but that was not allowed as the crew did all the stowing, the skipper acting as stevedore. Both schooners having finished loading at the same time, the merchant promised a new hat to the skipper who reached his destination first. Now we were going again from one climatic extreme to the other, Pernambuco being just south of The Line.

I should think St John's must be a very pleasant place in the summer, but it was the very opposite while we were there, although the inhabitants were very kind and hospitable, vying with each other in entertaining us after the day's work was done.

After leaving St John's together the schooners lost sight of each other until they arrived at the port of discharge. The other vessel got there a day before us, so I presume their skipper got the new hat. What reward our skipper got for being a day behind I do not know, but it ought to have been something more substantial than a hat as during the 24 hours difference in arrival times fish went up at a rate of five shillings a hundredweight.

It was terribly hot. So hot, indeed, that we worked the cargo at night. After discharging the fish, we started to load sugar for the United Kingdom. That was about the hardest job I had all the time I was at sea. We were lying off in the middle of the harbour, the cargo being loaded by day into barges which we had to tow off to the ship and tow the empty barges back again. For all the loading was done by the crew.

We were about three weeks in Pernambuco and we were not sorry to get away from there. What with the heat and the smell it was anything but a desirable place to stay in.

---

him to make up the wasted weeks, he seems to have decided a more leisurely route via Bermuda would suffice.

3   What with the shaking in the gale and the sharp contrast of climate during the voyage, the champagne must have been extremely well stowed to have survived!

After being at sea about a week we ran short of oil, it having been overlooked or forgotten by the skipper, but we soon got a supply from a very unexpected source. For we ran into a school of porpoises and it did not take us long to get the harpoon to work. Soon we had three of the beasts on deck. Fine, big fellows they were too, weighing about half a ton each. When we came to cut the blubber from them we found it about six inches thick, so there was plenty of oil in sight!

We set the cook to work at once to render the blubber down and by the next day we had a good supply of excellent oil as well as fresh meat which was very good. After cutting the blubber off we hung one of the carcasses up to the forestay for cutting steaks from. But, sad to say, after hanging for a couple of days the cook thought it might go bad, so one night he covered it up. There was no mistake about its being bad then, for if you got to leeward of it you would almost be knocked down, the stench was so bad. It is very curious, but you can cut from a porpoise to the last bit if you do not cover it.

The cook hung the heads up in the galley to drain the oil from them. He told me he could get a very big price for it as the jewellers and watchmakers would give quite a large sum for any they can get for lubrication in their crafts.

When we were about halfway on our passage we thought there was something wrong with our reckoning, for we were in sight of land when we should have been quite three days from any. So the skipper got his glasses and had a look. In fact we all had a look and, sure enough, there was the peak of Pico, Tenerife, right ahead of us. Then the skipper goes below and has a look at the chart and after being absent about a quarter of an hour comes on deck looking more puzzled than ever. For we were just where we ought to be, according to the day's reckoning. It was when the sun went down that we found out the trouble. For with that our "land" disappeared. It was a mirage. Anyway we kept on our course and we sighted Tenerife three days afterwards.

We duly arrived at Falmouth where we had to call for orders, and after lying there a week received our sailing instructions for Greenock: almost another voyage. There I left the ship on 8 July 1870, and proceeded to Bristol where, having rather a small pay day, I could not stay very long before getting to sea again.

9

We live on the Nile. The Nile we love,
By night we sleep on the cliffs above,
By day we fish and at eve we stand
On long, bare islets of yellow sand.
— Edward Lear

Money was getting short, so I had to look for a ship. Going to the shipping office for inquiries I saw on the shipping list that a vessel was wanting men, so I steered my way to the docks and after looking around a bit found her under the loading tip taking in a cargo of patent fuel[1] and coal, the fuel being loaded first with the coal on top.

She was a fine brigantine named *Sagitta* and was built in Guernsey in 1856. She was 302 tons register with a length of 135 feet and a beam of 25 feet. So I went aboard and had an interview with the skipper, arranging to sign on with the rest of the crew next day – 3 August 1870 – for a voyage to Alexandria, Egypt.

In those days it was quite the custom to load a vessel with as much as she could carry, the Plimsoll Loading Act[2] not having been passed then as to how much freeboard should be allowed. So on leaving dock I noticed that she was loaded almost to the scuppers: that is, a few inches from the level of the deck. Fortunately it was fine weather when we crossed the Bay of Biscay or we should have had a rough time of it.

When we arrived at our port of discharge the stevedores came aboard almost before we had made the ship fast to start with the cargo as it appeared the owners of it were quite without patent fuel. In this port the consignee found the labour to work the hold and the crew worked on deck discharging the baskets as they came up.

One morning as we were loading the barges we heard a lot of barracking and shouting. So, looking over the side we saw two magnificent gondolas coming down the

---

1   Coal dust mixed with a binding agent and pressed into brickettes.

2   Samuel Plimsoll (1824–1898) came from Bristol. As MP for Derby he campaigned for better conditions for seamen. In consequence, the Merchant Shipping Act of 1876 demanded the maximum loading line for vessels to be marked on hulls. The Plimsoll line is still used.

Nile loaded with the Pasha's[3] harem. There were about 24 of them, all very gaily dressed, but with their faces covered, so you could not see what they were like as regards looks.

We had a little fun while we were at Alexandria going ashore and having donkey rides, which seemed to be the only sport there was to be had there. However, it was great fun, the donkeys galloping all the time with boys behind them brandishing sticks with which they belaboured the beasts of burden when they slackened their pace.

I almost got into trouble one Sunday afternoon as we were having a ride to see the Sphinx. We were almost opposite with a crowd of natives watching us when my donkey knocked down a little boy. Whether it was the boy's mother or not, I don't know, but a lady in the crowd picked up a large stone and threw it at me. It missed me, but struck the donkey a nasty whack on its hindquarters causing him to rear up and almost pitch me off his back. At the same time he galloped at his hardest, soon getting out of the way of the irate woman.

Having finished discharging we had to sweep the hold out clean to take in a large cargo of cotton seed, the crew working it from the quay to the hatchway and native labour then trimming and treading it down in the hold. The treading was done by about 20 men walking and stamping it down as they walked. Loading completed, we set sail bound for Gloucester at which port we arrived in about eight days: that is, Sharpness as we had to go up the canal before we arrived at our destination. I stayed there a few days after signing off on 22 December 1870, and then took a run in a vessel to Newport which was going there to load, so I saved my passage money.

I kicked my heels ashore for something above a month when I found myself back in Bristol at my old lodgings. There I heard of a Guineaman[4] looking for crew. She was the *Bolivia*, a 378-ton vessel, 147 feet in length with a 25-foot beam. She had been built in Whitehaven in 1857. So I goes out to look for her and finds her lying at Redcliffe Wharf. She was having her sails bent, which were Colling and Pinkney Patent, so there would be no going aloft to stow or reef sails, all being done from the deck. The main jib was also patent, being wound round the stay like a blind on a roller. As regards the jib, I would much rather stow that in the ordinary way as it was continually getting jammed.[5] Going on board, I asked one of the riggers when she was signing on as I could see she was almost ready. This was Monday and he told me that the skipper was shipping crew on the Wednesday, 8 February 1871.

---

3   A local governor or senior official; strictly speaking, a Turkish term.

4   A ship trading to and from the Guinea Coast of West Africa, formerly notorious for the slave trade, but by Jack's time palm oil was the usual commodity shipped home in exchange for trade goods.

5   Colling and Pinkney's roller reefing for square-rigged sails was introduced during the second half of the 19th century. It saved labour aloft and the weight of heavy spars in conventional rigging. The sails could be furled by steam winch or by hand from the deck. Modern leisure sailors will sympathise with the frustration of roller reefed fore-and-aft sails jamming as this is a regular occurrence even on the most up-to-date sailing craft nowadays.

Chapter 9

The Bolivia *took Tom Sullivan to West Africa for new adventures. This painting was made of the ship outward bound on a voyage off St Donat's Head, by the accomplished French artist, Edouard Adam, in 1891*

"What do you want to know for?" he asks. "Are you wanting to ship in her?"

"Well, I'd thought about it."

"Oh, you did, did you? Because there are not many men who care about going to the west coast of Africa and I doubt if the skipper will get all his men without some trouble."

That sounded cheerful.

You see, the west coast of Africa had a very bad name being such a fever-stricken place, which I was to know more about later on. There were very few ships went out there that returned without losing some of the crew from the fever.[6] However, I turned up at the shipping office on the Wednesday and, although I did not like the look of the skipper – Captain J.O. Langdon – much, I signed on.

When I got back to the boarding house my landlady was very anxious to know if I had shipped.

"Yes," says I. "And we leave Bathurst Basin on Saturday morning's tide. Now, I shall give you my advance note and in return you must let me have some money to get a few things with." She didn't care much for that, but I told her that if she refused I should take the note somewhere else. With that she let me have what I required: about 30 shillings I think it was.

So having thanked her I says: "Could you put my half pay in the bank while I'm away, so that I can get interest on it?"

"Oh yes," she says. "I should be only too pleased to oblige you."

As the lady had treated me very well while I was staying with her – and not knowing much about honesty – I was foolish enough to leave her my half pay to place in the bank. She assured me it would be quite safe and waiting for me when I returned.

We shall see …

---

6   Malaria was the main culprit, passed on through the bites of mosquitoes that thrived in the coastal mangrove swamps. The Gambia River, further north, now a playground for tourists, was once so rife with malaria that it is believed to be the origin of the term "the white man's grave".

10

So geographers, in Afric-maps,
With savage pictures fill their gaps;
And o'er uninhabitable downs
Place elephants for want of towns.

—Jonathan Swift

So the following Saturday saw me leave Bristol for more than a year until April 1872. Whether I would come back again was the question in my mind, if all that rigger told me had any truth in it.

Just before we left the basin there were two butts of ale put aboard from Redcliffe Brewery for use until we got to sea. This was to make up for the fact that no fire was allowed in the galley until about 50 tons of gunpowder had been shipped and stowed away, which was to be taken on board at Curtis and Harvey's[1] down the river. All the crew had to work in their stockinged feet while the powder was about on account of their boots having nails in them which might have sparked.

We got to Kingroad and cleared up the ship a bit while lying at anchor. Then the pilot came aboard to see us down the Channel as far as Lundy Island where we dropped him. On the departure of the pilot the skipper called all hands aft to pick the watches. The skipper chose his man first, then the mate and so on until the watches were completed. Of course the steward, cook, carpenter and cooper were left out.

After he had settled about the watches and before he dismissed us, the skipper thought he would give us a little homily. So he starts with the following:

"Now men, before you leave the quarter deck I want you to understand that I am in command of this ship and when I say that I want a thing done I want it done at once and mean to be obeyed."

---

1   Curtis and Harvey was a gunpowder mill. Before more sophisticated chemicals were developed to demolish people and property, the volatile mixture of carbon, sulphur and saltpetre that was gunpowder served civil and military purposes.

With this little speech he finished by telling us:

"You can make this a good ship or a hell at sea. Now you can go for'ard."

Up to now I had never experienced anything of that kind, but I am sorry to say that the skipper soon started on the "hell" part of it himself. We had been out about two weeks and were just getting into the Tropics when the skipper thought the decks required something to whiten them up a bit. So he sent the mate for'ard one fine afternoon to inform all hands that they had to get on with holystoning the decks. That meant the watch whose turn it was to go below had to stay on deck at work instead of being in their bunks. As all commands from the skipper had to be obeyed there was nothing for it but to get on with the holystoning.

Holystones are blocks of freestone (fine sandstone or limestone) about the size of an ordinary brick and are used instead of brushes for scrubbing the deck, to give it an extra smoothness and whiteness. The crew had no objection to the work, but they did to being kept on deck when they ought to have been below. So the next day, when the officer of the watch ordered the crew to get on with scrubbing the decks and sent a man down the forepeak to get the stones, there were no stones to be found. They had been thrown overboard during the night.

When the skipper was told he came for'ard in a rare old paddy, demanding of the crew the name of the man who had buried the stones at sea. As nobody seemed to know, nobody could tell him.

Then I thought he was going to have a fit, he was in such a rage, but all his blustering did not get him the required information. So he ordered us all aft on to the poop and as soon as he could calm himself a bit he started to let us know how he was going to "punish us", as he said.

"You will be put on your 'pound and pint' for the rest of the passage to Cape Palmas. Now you can go for'ard and see how you like that!"

I do not recall full details of what the seaman's allowance was exactly, but I do remember that the worst part of it was you were allowed only three quarts of water a day for all purposes. So to be rationed to so small a quantity of water, especially in the Tropics, was about the cruellest thing the skipper could have thought of. Why, you want a quart to drink alone.

You see, in the usual order of things aboard ship, if any of the crew refused to obey the lawful commands of the ship's officers they could be "logged": that is, their offence was entered in the log book and they could be punished when the ship returned home. But in this case the crew never disobeyed the officers. They simply could not do the work because there was nothing to do it with. Anyway, we stopped having to endure the afternoon watch business.

The skipper went ashore when we reached Cape Palmas and when he came aboard again he gave orders that the watches were to go on as usual, and with that we got under way and made for the trading ports, if I may call them such.

We traded with a few small places, giving out goods on trust to be paid for when the ship returned down coast. The first place where we reckoned to do a big trade was Half Jack [Half Assini, Ghana], which was our next stopping place. But, you see, there was to be a settlement of some grievances which the chiefs had against the skipper. It appeared that on the previous voyage, just as the ship was about to set sail for home, there was a squabble with some of the natives about their pay and they refused to leave the ship. However, as she was already moving they all were forced to jump overboard … except one. He flatly refused to budge, whereupon the skipper hit him on the head with a horse pistol, tipping him over the rail at the same time and thus killing him. We were told all this by the natives themselves when we called there on the downward passage.

Before we had dropped anchor and as we were just clewing up the sails a canoe came off with three of the chiefs who came aboard and at once asked for the skipper. One of the chiefs had owned as a bondsman the fellow who had been killed and he was the first to tackle the skipper on the subject as soon as the latter appeared on the poop. They had not been talking many minutes before one of the other chiefs, who had not yet joined in the palaver, gave a signal to somebody ashore. A few minutes afterwards four of their largest canoes were seen putting off the beach. During this time the palaver was getting a bit hot.

I was on the poop at the time and heard the chiefs threaten what they would do if the skipper did not accede to what they demanded. His answer finally was to tell the steward to hand up a riding whip (whips of all sorts were part of the cargo) with which he belaboured one of the chiefs. He did not have time to use the whip much before he was collared by the three. One had hold of him round the neck, another by the waist and the third by the legs. They then proceeded to bundle him over the poop rail, he yelling out all the time for the crew to come to his assistance. But nobody attempted to lift so much as a finger towards helping him in any way.

By this time the four canoes had come alongside and about 300 natives swarmed aboard. The skipper, meanwhile, was being pitched overboard. He held on to the poop rail to try to save himself, but they rapped his knuckles with the handles of their knives and soon had him in the water where the canoe that had brought the chiefs off had been waiting all the time the melee was going on. Having got him to the canoe, they tore all his clothes off and beat him with their paddles, taking him ashore in Nature's garb.

The chiefs were still aboard – and a very good thing they were. For the crowd was pitching everything they could lay their hands on overboard and the crew were expecting to be attacked at any minute. If we had been, we had no means of defending ourselves and would have been overcome in a few minutes. But the chiefs prevented the natives from molesting the crew, telling us that they had no quarrel with us; it was only the captain they wanted.

They sought out the mate and told him he could anchor if he wished and no harm would be done to him or any of the crew, or he could continue on his way. They seemed quite satisfied with the capture of the skipper. The mate was for dropping the anchor, but his crew would not agree to that as they argued that the chiefs might change their minds. So, as the sails were only clewed up, we hauled the sheets home again, starting once more on our journey up the coast.

When the skipper was taken ashore the chiefs said they were going to take him into the bush and leave him there, but – fortunately for him – there happened to be another barque lying off Half Jack which hailed from the same port, the captain of which was much liked by the natives who would do almost anything to please him. So when he saw our skipper being brought ashore in such disarray with the three chiefs, he knew there must be something very much amiss. He hurried up to get alongside the canoe before she was beached to see what the trouble was. After having a long palaver with the chiefs he managed to prevent them from taking our skipper into the bush, but they would not let him go scot free.[2] They intended to punish him and punish him they did.

They shut him up in a hut with a strong guard over him. The next morning they had him out on to the beach and put him in the sand up to his hips then set the women on to beat him with wet sheets. That not being enough, they dosed him with chilli peppers, putting them anywhere they could about the tenderest parts of his naked person to give him pain. When they took him from the ship they declared they would kill him and if it had not been for the other skipper's intercession I believe they would have done so.

It appeared that when the chiefs boarded our ship and saw the skipper they demanded "trust": that is, goods on credit for all those who belonged to the chief who lost the native. Of course, the value of the goods would have been paid for in palm oil, ivory and so on when the ship called next time, but the skipper would not agree to anything of the kind. So he endangered the lives of the whole crew by his stubbornness. For if the chiefs had been anything like him there was nothing to stop us being massacred as the natives swarmed on deck.

We were away about a week and as soon as the anchor was down when we brought up again at Half Jack the same chiefs came aboard with the skipper. My word. What a pitiable object he looked as he came on the poop where he had to stay until he had satisfied all the natives' requirements. Then the chiefs had everything that was looted from the ship given up. The things were brought alongside in a separate canoe. As the canoes were leaving and the last native was going over with his chief the cooper came along and, seeing his cap on the blackamoor's head, pointed it out to his chief, who snatched it off and threw the fellow overboard.

Before we left Half Jack we took a dozen krooboys[3] aboard to help work the ship. They were very useful when we were taking oil on board.

---

2   An ancient tax levied by a lord on his subjects. To be let off scot free was to be exempt from such a tax. This later came to mean being let off anything one might have been expected to pay in dues of cash or kind.

3   A word dating from 1835 in English usage. Krooboys were Liberians from a coastal tribe skilled in seamanship. They were recruited for their local knowledge to work on ships plying the West African trade.

Everything being settled, we set sail up the coast again, stopping at the trading places as we went along. The skipper always managed to do the sailing at night so as to have the whole of the next day for working the cargo. It was quite a week before he was able to show up on deck, doing his business down below with the help of the steward. As he got better he resumed his bullying tactics and tyrannising of the crew.

When the ship was at anchor at night it was customary to have one man to keep watch, but the skipper said two could keep watch better than one. So for the rest of the trading part of the voyage two were kept on the anchor watch.

It was quite a sight to see our departure from Half Jack. There were four of the large canoes with about a hundred natives in each and as we were heaving up the anchor they paddled around the ship singing and gesticulating, the chiefs joining in as they stood on the poop. Then as the vessel started to move they all turned towards the beach, the canoe with the goods on board leading the way.

What a difference it was to our arrival there on the outward passage.

11

What lasting joys the man attend
who has a polished female friend.

— **Cornelius Whurr**

We had been out about six months now and were fairly busy when I was struck down with fever and ague. So I was confined to my bunk for about eight weeks, but with the aid of the medicine chest and the steward – who was an excellent nurse – I got round again all right.

When I got on deck again I found there had been changes made in the victualling department. Instead of a pound of bread a day we had a pound of plantain which – when the skins were taken off – was rather over a quarter pound short in weight.

Should any reader not know what a plantain is, I will explain. It is quite a familiar fruit now in England, but spoken of generally as "bananas". Now, a banana is not much bigger than your middle finger, whereas a plantain is about three times that size when fully-grown. I've seen a few bananas in England, but not many and they are imported mostly from the Canary Islands. What we do get here are half-grown plantains from the West Indies.

For our Sunday dinners we had a whole pig as near the weight of the crew's requirements as the steward could guess, the pig being weighed by spring balance just as it was, trotters and entrails included. Then it was cut in half, one side for each watch. When dinner time came, the half pig was cut up into pieces as equal as the cook could manage to make them for each man to have his proper share. Then one of the crew stood at the fo'castle hatch and called the name of each of his fellows, at the same time sticking his fork into one of the pieces and handing it down until all had been served.

While we were lying off Cape Three Points [Ghana] which was as far as our activities extended to leeward (we only traded on the weather coast) it came to our turn to go to Cape Palmas for the mails, which event happened every three months, each vessel taking it in turns. There were generally four or five ships lying off Cape Three Points. So me and the second mate were told off to make the journey of nearly 400 miles in the longboat.[1] It was rather a risky job, but as the only danger was from the shore, we could easily avoid that by keeping well out to sea.

Our crew consisted in two krooboys – one for each watch – then, having taken our provisions aboard, we also shipped a "devil" to cook with: that is, a sort of grate made with hoop iron. We also took an 18-gallon cask of water, not forgetting a Colt[2] revolver each for me and the mate.

We were starting to push off when the skipper handed the second mate a note which was not to be opened until we had been away for two days. We pushed off wondering what mystery there was attached to the note. But we obeyed the instructions and left opening the missive until the third day of leaving the ship.

When I saw the look on the mate's face I couldn't help laughing; he looked so serious.

"Just read that, Jack," says he, "and see what you think about it."

The contents were that we were not to forget to call off Grand Bassam [Ivory Coast] and pick up a lady whom the chief of Cape Three Points had bought for a wife.

"Well," I says, "that's nothing to be upset about, is it?"

"Oh ain't it?" he retorts. "What about these two niggers?"

He went on to talk about returning to the ship.

"There will be no trouble with them when they see a revolver pointing at them," I says. "So don't you worry, but keep on with the voyage."

As we went along we closed in on the shore now and again to buy some fresh provisions. The skipper had given us some heads of tobacco to trade with. We procured fowls, eggs, fruit and so on, and also some plantains and palm wine. The latter is a splendid drink. It is obtained by puncturing the oil palm tree. Then the liquid will run quite freely and yield nearly two gallons before having to be plugged. We always took the precaution of making the natives drink of it first before taking it on board.

We got along all right, barring a tornado or two, which the boat weathered splendidly.

---

1   See glossary. Modern health and safety officials would blanch at such a hazardous enterprise, although such trips in the open longboat to pick up the mails were clearly routine.

2   American Samuel Colt was an inventor from a young age and the father of the revolving pistol, which delivered a series of rounds to the firing chamber of the gun by way of a revolving wheel. Patented in 1835, the Colt revolver mechanism reached the zenith of its fame (with a little help later from Hollywood) as an essential tool in the taming of the Wild West of America. In reality, although Colt's weapons were marvellous machines, even they could not withstand the neglect of cowboys who had more interest in their four-legged charges than cleaning and maintaining their six-shooters. As a result, an as often as not mis-firing pistol would do more harm to the firer than to his target. Those unfortunate enough to be hit by a Colt round in the West were more likely to die of infection from grime on the bullet than the effects of the wounding itself.

Chapter 11

One day I thought we would have a hot dinner. So having bought some shallots I made a few doughboys and put them in the pot with some bully beef and a couple of plantains cut up, installing one of the natives as cook.

But, as the mainsail was abaft the "galley", I could not keep my eye on him very well. So when dinner time came I found three of the doughboys missing. I had made eight.

"Here, you nigger! What have you done with them doughboys, eh?" I cries.

"Me no eat 'em. Me only taste 'em to see if they'm done," he replies.

"Very well," says I. "As you've tasted so much, you'll have no need of a dinner."

But I gave him the remains after we had finished for he cooked it very well.

When we arrived at Cape Palmas the mate went ashore for the mails which turned out to be rather heavy, there being so many parcels and cases. But we managed to stow them away safely out of the way of the weather and seas. We lay off the harbour for a couple of days then made sail for Cape Three Points. We were rather anxious to get to Grand Bassam to see what our passenger was like.

As we approached there we could see a canoe putting off to meet us, the natives crewing the canoe singing for all they were worth as they paddled. I suppose they were singing a farewell to the maiden they were bringing away from her home. They came alongside with their precious cargo which turned out to be two ladies, the bride and her maid, which caused more anxiety to the mate.

When we had got them aboard and very carefully placed them in what was to be their berth until they arrived at their destination, we found that when their sheets were removed they were covered with various coloured stripes of some kind of grease so that their purchaser could see if they had been tampered with on the voyage. We noticed the two krooboys having a good look at them and talking to themselves, so the mate went for'ard and warned them of what they would get should they attempt to molest our cargo.

Our passengers certainly did not intend to starve during the journey. For they brought an abundance of food with them: yams, plantains, a couple of fowls and a quantity of eggs. The girls also told the men in the canoe that delivered them to take our water cask ashore and bring it back full.

We did not have much trouble as far as the krooboys were concerned. The mate did catch one of them crawling aft to where the ladies were one night. He had thought the mate was asleep until he felt the muzzle of a revolver in the middle of his back.

Two days after leaving Grand Bassam we sighted our ship and signalled the skipper notifying that we had the prospective bride aboard with her handmaid. The chief had been advised some time before when our skipper had seen us about an hour's sail off. So he was alongside the ship in his canoe about the same time as we were and was able to see that the "goods" were all right before delivery. He was very pleased as he looked his lady over from the top of her head to the soles of her feet. Then he went aboard the ship to have a palaver with the skipper, but it was not long before he came on deck again with a smile all over his face and got into the canoe with his new purchase to take her to his "castle".

After that was all over we had to deliver the mails to the other ships. Then we got back to our ship to resume our everyday duties.

12

It is the wisdom of the crocodiles,
that shed tears when they would devour.

— **Francis Bacon**

While we were away in the longboat the skipper had purchased an alligator about eight feet in length which he said he was going to present to the Zoological Gardens,[1] the carpenter having made a trough to keep it in. How he intended to keep it on the passage home I do not know, especially as he bought half a dozen small ones to keep it company. I mention this because I want to show what nice things they are to have aboard ship!

After we had left Cape Three Points and were lying at anchor at our first stopping place it happened to be my first watch, about eight bells [midnight], when I took a stroll aft to see how the alligator was getting on with his chums. But I could not see anything of them. The big one had swallowed them all!

I resumed my watch, forgetting all about the alligators until I called the next watch, telling him about the missing youngsters, but he only laughed as we went to have another look. To our surprise and consternation we found that the big one had broken open the trough and escaped. As a second man came on deck to complete the new watch, I

---

1   Bristol Zoo Gardens were founded in 1835 by a group of eminent citizens of the city and opened to the public the next year. The zoo is the fifth oldest in the world and the oldest not in a capital city. There were 220 shareholders who subscribed the cash to buy the land and build the zoo. Some of the descendants of these original shareholders are still connected with the zoo. At the time Jack describes, the Zoo Gardens became a focus of social and recreational activity for the citizens of Bristol, as well as a place of serious zoological study. There were flower shows, band concerts and boat trips on the lakes, as well as tennis, croquet and archery tournaments. Zebi, the zoo's famous elephant, was there from 1868 to 1909 and Jack probably took his children to wonder at this exotic creature. It was as well not to get too close to her, though, for she had a reputation for removing and eating straw hats.

thought he would have a fit when we told him about the fugitive. However, we got a lantern and searched the deck all over, but we could not see anything of it, greatly to our relief. You see, the alligator was placed aft on the poop, lashed down to a couple of ring bolts, and as the poop was slanting, the beast must have slid into the water.

It took us some time to collect our cargo, the natives being in no great hurry to deliver the oil. At last we reached Half Jack again where we were to complete loading. We were no sooner at anchor than the canoes started to bring off the oil, paddling around the ship with the occupants singing before making fast alongside.

There were two – sometimes three – puncheons in each canoe. Now, a puncheon weighs about 15 hundredweight, so you may imagine the size of the canoes which were cut out from one tree, the cabbage tree[2] I believe it is called. It took 20 men to work or paddle such a craft, whichever the propelling method is called.

We were lying off this place about three weeks and busy taking on cargo all the time, which included ivory, gold, ebony and thousands of coconuts. Why it took us so long to load was because the skipper had put so much trust goods ashore that the chiefs had been collecting the cargo the whole time we were away. It says much for the honesty of the natives in those days, for the chiefs delivered the whole value of the goods they had on trust; moreover when we had finished loading and were ready to sail there was a very friendly palaver between the chiefs and the skipper. They took their departure with a nine-gallon cask of rum as a "souvenir". Then after they had paddled around the ship a couple of times they made for the beach.

We gave some very hearty shanties, I can assure you, as we hove up the anchor for the last time before sighting The Lizard.

There was just one incident I must mention that happened on the passage home. One day in the afternoon watch we were pointing[3] some ropes. While we were so occupied the skipper came up from below and strolled towards us. After watching us for a few minutes he started criticising one of the crew member's work which the said man objected to, telling the "bully" to go below and mind his own business.

"If you give me any of your cheek I'll kick you off the poop!" declares the skipper.

"Two can play at that game," the other retorts and with that knocked the skipper down with a tremendous blow under the jaw, saying at the same time: "Come on and do your kicking!"

But the skipper did not feel inclined to take up the invitation as he had as much as he could do to crawl down the poop into the cabin. After being below for about an hour he roused up the mate whose watch it was below and told him to bring down the man who had struck him and have him logged for mutiny.

We heard no more of the incident, but it certainly made things much more comfortable aboard for the rest of the passage home. Any complaint the skipper had to

2   Various exotic trees the foliage of which resembled a cabbage were dubbed by non-botanist observers "cabbage trees". This one was probably a large palm.

3   Probably splicing rope, using the point of a marlin spike, the tool for the purpose.

make against any of the crew after this fracas was made through one of the mates.

It was nearly three months after leaving Half Jack before we arrived in the Bristol Channel and a year and nine months altogether on the voyage. The next day after our arrival in port we went to the shipping office to get paid off and we were all expecting to see the police there to take the "mutineer" in charge, but nothing happened. We asked the mate the reason and he said the skipper had drawn his pen through the entry in the log book.

After being paid off I made my way straight to the landlady I had left my half pay with to find that she had spent the lot. Something over 20 pounds it was.

"Well," I says. "You've kept your word, haven't you?"

She did not know what to say, only sat down and cried until I told her I was not going to give her in charge. Then she found her tongue and told me that she had got married while I was away and started to blame her husband, a man who was earning about four pounds a week.[4]

To make restitution she brought forward her husband's watch and said I could stay with her until I went on my next voyage if I would not prosecute her. So I accepted the watch and told her she would have to board and lodge me for three months. With rather a bad grace she agreed to my terms.

Among my other voyages I returned to the West African coast on another occasion when I had more adventures, of which I shall tell you in a later chapter. Meanwhile I ask the reader to reflect on the remarkable aspect of a sailor's life which was unheard of among those toiling ashore in those days. Fancy coming home from the west coast of Africa, say, where the heat was melting, to sail away next to northern ports where there was no heat at all, so to speak.

---

4   The implication is that the couple were far from hard up, with the wife's lodging house earnings added to the husband's princely (to Jack) £4 a week. The writer's apparent slur on his landlady's new male companion and his comparative "wealth" lend more credence to the theory that Jack felt jilted and possibly jealous of this rival.

13

God made the wicked grocer
For a mystery and a sign,
That men might shun the awful shops
And go to inns to dine.

— G.K. **Chesterton**

What follows has nothing whatever to do with the sea, but it just shows what a variety of jobs a seaman will tackle.

Having arrived after a voyage once at Newport it struck me that I might get a job ashore, so I started to tramp again as I had on my eventful stroll from London to Liverpool some years earlier. This time my path traced a shorter route, to Chepstow, for I thought that there must be plenty of work there, or thereabouts, as the Severn Tunnel was being built then.[1] So I made my way to the tunnel works to see what chance there was of anything in the way of a job. I went to Caldicot first, but was told that all workmen were engaged at Portskewett, the site of the main shaft. So after a visit to an inn – The Old Tippling Philosopher[2] by name – for something to eat and drink, I made my way to Portskewett.

The foreman there told me on my inquiring if any hands were wanted that there was plenty of work, but only for navvies. As that was something I did not care for much as a job, I thanked him and made my way back to Chepstow. Walking along St Mary Street I was hailed by somebody who turned out to be a grocer. He asked if I was looking for work. I told him that was precisely what I had come to Chepstow for.

---

1   The Victorians considered the rail route from London to South Wales an important one, the only obstacle being the wide and tidal Severn estuary. So the four-mile (6.4-kilometre) Severn Tunnel was started in 1873 and opened in 1886. It was not without its difficulties. Six years into construction the Great Spring, an unanticipated underground watercourse, was breached and flooded the workings. This was not finally sealed until 1881.

2   The Old Tippling Philosopher dates back at least to 1801 and still exists. John Joseph and his son-in-law, Thomas Hicks, held the licence from 1857 to near the close of the century. They undoubtedly served Jack his food and drink.

Chapter 13

"Well," he says, "I'm in want of a hand. Do you know anything about grocery?"

I said I did not but I could soon get into it.[3]

"Do you know anything about horses and can you drive?" he goes on.

"Oh yes," says I, though I had only driven them when out pleasuring.

"Very well," says he. "I will give you a trial. Your work will be out in the warehouse. You will have nothing to do with the shop."

So that was settled and I was to start in the morning at the wage of 18 shillings a week.[4]

With that I left him and set about looking for lodgings. I was rather fortunate as the first lady I inquired of was quite willing – and even pleased – to accommodate me when I told her who I was going to work for and that the situation was a constant one. She agreed to do everything for me; I to find my food which she would cook ready for me as I came home, for which I was to pay two and sixpence a week.

I was up early next morning and after a good wash and making myself look a bit tidy I set off on my new venture, getting to the shop long before it was opened. Thus I had time to go round to the stables and get some sort of insight into the general working of them. The man whose place I was taking had to harness the pony for the traveller, so I had a good opportunity of seeing how he did it, making mental notes. There were two horses; a heavy one for delivering goods and the pony for the traveller.

I soon got into the work and after a couple of days was sent out with the other man to assist him and to be introduced to the customers. I got on very well in the way of mastering the work and seemed to give satisfaction to my new employer. However, I was anything but pleased with the turn of events I became embroiled in. Quite the other way about, in fact.

It so happened that a draper's shop was right opposite the grocer's where I was employed. After I had got my load of groceries up, the drapery proprietor would come across and ask me if I would deliver a few parcels on the way for him. This I did, not thinking that it was to be a regular thing, but the parcels very much increased in number – also very much in bulk. So I thought I had better have something to say in the matter.

I had been there about three weeks when, one afternoon, after I had finished getting my load up, Mr Draper[5] came along with his little lot on a brace of trucks. There was drapery as well as rolls of oilcloth and the like which he commenced to load up on my wagon. I did not say anything to him just then, but went into the grocer's shop and asked him who was going to pay me for delivering the draper's goods. Then the draper spoke up and said it was an arrangement between him and my employer that I should deliver

---

3   And so he did. His trade is given as grocer on his wedding certificate, when he was married in Bristol on 25 January 1874, which must have been shortly after these events.

4   This warehouseman's wage was approaching that of his Bristol landlady's husband, so Jack must have been reasonably satisfied.

5   Contemporary records show "Mr Draper" was undoubtedly Thomas Jones, linen and woollen draper. The grocer was either James Guest, William Lewis Hodgson or Walter Price Thomas, all of whom were in the same line of business in St Mary Street at the time.

any goods for him that did not take me out of my way. This was about five in the evening and I had to go a round of some seven miles or more.

I asked my employer if that was so and he said it was; also that all the men before me had done it and never complained.

"Well sir," says I. "I can assure you that I do not intend to do it, so you will please deliver the goods yourself as I am going home."

Next morning I went to see him to get what little money was due to me. He did not have much to say, but he gave me a very good character and with that I left him, making my way back to Newport after settling with my landlady, who seemed really sorry that I was leaving.

So I ended my shore-going venture.

14

The captain in his bunk,
drinking bottled ditchwater;
and the crew is gambling in the forecastle,
She will strike and sink and split …
— **George Bernard Shaw**

My travels were destined to take me to Africa again when I was looking for a berth in Bristol one day. By making inquiries at the shipping office I found that the firm of R. and W. King, of Redcliffe Wharf, wanted some runners to go to Liverpool and bring down a barque they had purchased: the *Lord Duncan*.[1]

So I managed to see the skipper and he gave me the chance of being one of the runners, especially as I had been out to the "Coast" before. For he said any men who brought the ship down could stay on board and get her ready for sea if they wished to. The ship happened to belong to the same firm as the other one I made my voyage in to the "Coast". So I had the pleasure of another six weeks ashore which very much pleased my old landlady.

The barque was eventually ready for sea, having been renovated from truck to keelson, including nearly all the copper sheathing on the outside of her hull. Most long-voyagers in those days were sheathed with Muntz's Metal,[2] a composition – I believe – of copper and brass, but this firm always used pure copper and the ships were sheathed right up to the loaded mark. She looked very smart as she lay in the dock waiting to sail. She must have cost a mint of money in her renovation. All her square sails were Colling and Pinkney's Patent, so the crew could reef and stow them without going aloft.

---

1   There is no Certificate of Discharge for this voyage, but it is referred to elsewhere in the interview with the *Bristol Times* in 1926 (see Appendix A). There can be little doubt that the *Lord Duncan* was the vessel the writer refers to here.

2   The inventor, G.F. Muntz, of Birmingham, patented Muntz's Metal in 1832 for protecting ships' bottoms from the ravages of worm and wear. It was an alloy of copper and zinc, though, not brass.

Liverpool, a few years before Tom Sullivan's birth
(courtesy of National Maritime Museum, Greenwich, London)

The crew having signed on and the tug waiting in the river, we set sail as before for Cape Palmas, stopping down the river to take in about 60 tons of gunpowder. This was to be a very different voyage from the first one I made to the west coast of Africa, our skipper being quite a gentleman. He rarely spoke to any of the crew. Anything he wished to say, or any complaint he wished to make, was always done through the officers.

So soon as we left Kingroad and the watches were picked, the skipper sent us forward saying that he hoped we should have a pleasant voyage and behave ourselves like men. Well, what a difference in tone to the dire warnings of a "hell ship" given to the crew of the ship on my first African passage! However, this skipper was delivering a kindlier version of the same message to us. That is, with a long voyage in prospect, the crew should prepare themselves for getting on with their tasks as well as getting on with each other for the considerable time they would spend within the confined space of the ship's accommodation.

On this voyage we did not do any trading on the weather coast, our first stopping place being Cape Coast Cassel; Benin being the limit. So you see we only traded in the Bight of Benin.

I am sorry to say that we had a few undesirables among the crew who were rather inclined to cut up rusty because others objected to their gambling instincts. When the ship lay at anchor and we were all down below they would bring out a pack of cards and play Euchre,[3] a game very much in fashion among seafaring men at that time, and keep it up all night. In between their playing and cursing the rest of us could get no sleep. This went on for some time until they thought of something to drink. This they got by breaking the bulkhead in the fo'castle and tapping a rum cask. Then, having got some of the fiery spirit in them, they made the place a perfect hell and our talking to them was like pouring water on a duck's back for all the notice they took of it.

Some of the crew suggested that we should tell the mate, but I said I thought it would be much better to do away with the cause of the trouble by destroying the cards, which I volunteered to do. So I watched where they hid the pack and at the first chance I got in the morning I put the wretched pasteboards in the galley fire.

You should have heard and seen them when they could not find their cards! The language they used and the epithets they flung at one another were nobody's business. All swore that they need not pay each other their gambling debts. They had played for their tobacco, wages, clothes and whatever else I could not say.

Anyway, the rest of us were able to get some sleep when we turned in. So that ended the first and only trouble we had during the voyage. Everything was forgotten by the gamblers in a few days. They did not have any desire for the rum, either.

While we were lying off Cape Coast, Gold Coast [Ghana], it happened to be my anchor watch one night when I saw what I was never to see again. That was a fight between a whale and a thresher shark. They were only a few yards from the ship. The whale was springing up quite eight feet from the water, the thresher lying in wait for it as it dropped. It was such a sight that I called the rest of the crew to see it. Each time the whale came down it was like a cannon going off. One of the natives told me that the thresher never leaves the whale until it has killed it.

After trading at a few small places – you could not call them ports – we came to Accra, Gold Coast, one of the principal ports in the Bight of Benin, which I believe it is still. We had dropped anchor when the skipper sent the mate forward to tell us that he intended we should all have a day on shore as we would be lying off there some considerable time. We were to go ashore in couples.

But, alas for the frailty of human nature, only one couple went ashore and they were brought back aboard that night thoroughly soaked – on their insides at least – and speechless. They had to be hauled up on board like bundles of rags. So that ended the liberty we were all about to get.

While we lying at Accra the mail boat put a quantity of provisions and so on aboard for one of a Liverpool firm's agents. These goods proved a great nuisance as we continually had to shift them about the hold to get at what we required from time to time.

---

3   Euchre is an American card game dating from the 1840s. The deuces, threes, fours, fives and sixes are discarded leaving a 32-card pack for play. A player may pass, but if he chooses to play his turn he must take three tricks or forfeit two points. The highest card is the knave of trumps (Right Bower). The other knave of the same colour is the second-highest card (Left Bower).

One day we were very busy when the krooboys thought they were entitled to a drink. So one of them asked the second mate – who had charge of the work in the hold – to give them something to quench their thirst. This is what he said in answer to their request:

"Look here, you animated lumps of charcoal, I'll see you in hell as far as you are out of it and the door locked and the key lost with the Devil on holiday and not expected back for three weeks and even then you won't get one drop!"

"Oh, mister mate, just a little drop!"

"Not half a drop. And if you don't clear out I'll put my toe on your arse and kick you overboard!"

The thirsty krooboys cleared out …

At about five next morning we heard a terrible hullabaloo going on among the krooboys and, thinking they had all got at the rum, we hurried on deck. Looking over the starboard rail we saw six of the boys in the water. They had got hold of a large turtle and were trying to turn it on its back and push it towards the ship. So what with the shouting of the boys in the water together with that of their brothers on deck it was a regular pandemonium.

They got the turtle aboard at last and it was a large one. I think it would have turned the scales at between four or five hundredweight. When they cut it open they got out three ship's buckets full of eggs from it. The eggs are without shells, but have a sort of parchment skin and are nearly round in shape. As none of the crew cared to taste turtle the boys had it all to themselves. It lasted them about three days, so it must have been a very large one as there were 12 krooboys. I think the skipper had the shell as a souvenir of the voyage.

We were now about three parts loaded and looking forward to going home. We whetted our appetite for the return trip by making calculations as to how long it would be before we sailed. Then, lo and behold, one fine morning we saw the skipper signalling the mail boat. We were lying off Lagos, Nigeria, at the time. We had no idea as to what the signalling was about, but we were very soon to know when we were ordered to get the main hatches off and haul a hundred puncheons of oil up and trans-ship them to the mail boat. That knocked our calculations as to when we should be homeward bound into a cocked hat and our faces went very long, I can tell you. We had now been out about 12 months and breaking cargo of a hundred puncheons meant quite another six weeks before we should be able to do any more calculating about going home.

The downcast mood of the crew was not improved by a rather sad thing which occurred on board at this time. One of our number went down with the fever and in two or three days went almost mad. So bad was he that the skipper had him berthed aft out of the way of the men and the noise of working the ship. As the unfortunate patient made several attempts to get on deck, we had to make him fast to the bunk. One day I went to attend to him and found him lying full length on the deck. How he got clear of the lashings was a mystery. Anyhow, I had to get him back into his bunk.

He was a very tall man, but I managed to get him on his feet and placed him with his back against the bunk which was an upper one. Then I took hold of his legs to tip him over when something went "crack!" which made me give a jump as I thought I had broken him in two. I had a fright and no mistake, but I felt him all over – he talking to his friends the while – and found no bones broken, for which I was heartily thankful as I thought I might have killed him.

As I had been through a similar bout of illness I was only too glad to take on the nurse's job in all the spare time I had. I am pleased to say the patient got quite well after about four months, two months of which he was on his back. That was the only case of sickness we had during the whole voyage.

At last we were at anchor off Cape Coast again where we were to finish loading. This took about a fortnight, all the cargo being ready for us to take on board. Although we had sent so much on before, there was a large quantity had to be left behind when we sailed for home.

We had been at sea about two weeks and were just getting out of the doldrums about half a degree of Latitude north of the Line when a strange thing happened. It was a very fine night, the moon and stars being quite brilliant. I was at the wheel when the lookout shouted:

"Ship on the weather bow!"

It seemed very curious, for the vessel appeared to be going about six knots with the wind abeam, but put the helm how I would, I could not see how I was to clear her.

She was a fine, full-rigged ship – one of the tea clippers, I should think – and she made a beautiful sight with the moon shining on her sails. The scene would have made a fine picture.

We were going stern-on to her, for whichever way I put the helm she would still seem to be in the same position. All at once I had a great shock, for the look-out was yelling for all he was worth that we had run her down as she had disappeared entirely.

Now, as I had felt no shock and there were no men or debris to be seen in the water, it was quite evident that we had not run into anything. It was a cloud that came over the face of the moon which caused the ship's disappearance. In fact it was nothing but a mirage – the second one I had seen in as many years – but nothing to the one I was going to see later on during a voyage through the Mediterranean.

We were having a splendid passage home and nothing untoward happened until we got into the Channel. Then a gale set in from the east – a regular sneezer – and try how we could, the skipper could not make the Bristol Channel. It was nothing but "about ship!" all the time with close-reefed topsails, but the vessel made very fine weather of it, shipping very little water. So we were not troubled much with having to use the pumps. However, the wind was on the change and dropped considerably, so we were able to put on more sail. As the wind had got to the southward a bit we steered for the Bristol Channel.

We had been knocking about for three weeks, but I cannot say any of us were sorry as we had a good ship and plenty of grub, so we were very well satisfied with things as they were. And, as I have said before: "more days, more dollars"!

At last we sighted Lundy and there we found a tugboat on the lookout for us. The skipper had signalled The Lizard a few days before, so the owners were advised of our presence in the Channel. We had no sooner got off Lundy when the winds veered round to the south-west and started to blow a gale. So we had to put the ship under close-reefed topsails again. Even then the tug could not catch up to us, for we were doing about eight knots, the wind being on the beam. When we got off Weston-super-Mare the tug managed to pick us up at last, but we could not save the tide, so we had to drop anchor in Kingroad to wait for the next one.

The people had got news of the arrival of a Guineaman in the roads and when we arrived at Cumberland Basin there were hundreds of them on the quay waiting to give us a welcome, it being the ship's first voyage for her new owners. We had been away about 14 months and, considering the trade the skipper had done, I think it must have been a very profitable voyage. As I had not been so foolish as to leave any half pay for anyone to bank for me, being bitten so badly before, I had a nice little pay day, so was able to have a good time ashore, not thinking of going to sea again until the money was gone.

So it was nearly four months before I started to look for a ship.

15

Oh, I am a cook and a captain bold,
And the mate of the Nancy brig,
And a bo'sun tight, and a midshipmite,
And the crew of the captain's gig.

— W.S. Gilbert

W alking along the quay in Bristol one morning some years later, in July 1883, a smart little craft caught my eye. She was evidently getting ready for sea. She was the 177-ton schooner *A.D. Gilbert*, registered in Falmouth having been built in Truro in 1865 by Hodge's. Her length was 108 feet and her beam 23 feet. The skipper was Captain Henry Langford.

The mate being on the quarter deck mending a sail, I hailed him and made inquiries as to when she sailed and if she had got her full crew.

"Yes," he says. "I think we have, if they all show up at the shipping office, except the cook and steward. Is that the berth you want?"

I told him that was just the job I was looking for.

It being a Saturday, he then tells me: "We sign on, all being well, on Monday. The skipper has just gone ashore, but I daresay you will do. So if you will give me your word that you will be at the shipping office with your discharges on Monday morning about ten o'clock I will tell the skipper as soon as he comes aboard."

Then I asks: "Where are you bound for?"

"Well," says he, "we go over to Newport first to load and then sail to Smyrna [Izmir] in Turkey; a nice little trip."

So, on Monday morning I shows up at the shipping office rather early as I wanted to see the captain and have a word or two with him before signing on. He was a gentlemanly-looking man, not much like a seaman in appearance. There was some peculiarity about him that I could not quite put my finger on. I found out after we had been at sea a few days that he was what you might call a little bit "touched". Otherwise he was a very good skipper as well as a clever one.

We set sail from Newport on the Thursday morning[1] with a good breeze which lasted until we got just to the south'ard of Ushant. Then it fell to a dead calm. As we were then in the Bay of Biscay I experienced something that I had never come across before: that was what we called at sea "Atlantic rollers". There was no wind and the water was like glass. The vessel was sliding, as it appeared, down the mountain side of water and up another. The water would come right up to the taffrail before receding and it looked as if she was going down nose-first until you saw her start climbing the next roller. It was a lovely night and you could see the moon shining beautifully in every mountainous wave.

We only had a few hours of that before a breeze sprang up from the north and we were able to get on, which we did with all sail set and going about eight knots. The wind kept up and we arrived at Gibraltar where about a dozen vessels were going through "The Funnel" as the skipper called the Strait of Gibraltar. We were the only ship under canvas among the lot of them and now I was to see what the little schooner could do.

When we entered the strait with a stiff breeze blowing I should think we were going about 10 knots. What speed the steam tramps were able to do I did not know. It was about eight bells in the first watch at night [midnight] when we entered the strait and about the same time next morning [4 a.m.] we were in the Mediterranean without a tramp in sight. We had out-sailed all of them! But with the wind falling off they caught us up one after the other as wind made no difference to their sailing.

We had not got as far as Minorca when we were caught in a gale and had to shorten sail, which delayed us somewhat. But as it was a westerly gale we were able to make pretty fair progress. It got a bit calmer after a few hours and we were not troubled again until we got to the Grecian Isles, when we seemed to have nothing but a succession of gales on a small scale.

We were off one of the largest of the islands (I forget the name of it) with very little wind when there was a great upheaval of the sea. We were tossed about horribly, but shipped no water. The skipper said he had an idea that there must have been an earthquake on one of the islands which also affected the sea. When we got to Smyrna we found out that such was the case, the earthquake being terrible, resulting in the loss of about 3000 lives. All the fishing vessels that were inshore were also destroyed, with the loss of most of their crews. There has been some similar disaster since, I think, but none so destructive as that.

We were now getting close to our destination, so we started getting ready for discharging cargo as soon as we got into port, which we did a week after leaving Gibraltar. I found Smyrna to be a very busy place. There was plenty of shipping there, mostly large

---

1   The trip across the Bristol Channel seems to have been counted as a "run" by the clerk in the shipping office who made up Jack's Certificate of Discharge in Dublin at the end of this voyage, for the signing-on date is given as 12 July 1883, a Thursday. Or perhaps the skipper was not so "touched" when it came to saving on sailors' pay by counting the trip from Newport, as the paper shows, and not Bristol.

sail boats as well as tramp steamers. They have very fine docks and do a big trade. The North German Lloyd's and the Austrian Lloyd's were very much in evidence. We were berthed alongside an English tramp, one of the Bank Line from London, owners of the schooner I was in as well. Ours was the only vessel they possessed under canvas, the skipper told me.

At Smyrna work is carried out day and night. There are rails laid out all round the quays which are used for passenger as well as goods trains by day and all goods by night. The railways and the trains were under the control of the French government in those days. Each morning the railway lines would be full of trucks with various merchandise, mostly barley. Then there was the camel traffic. It was very strange when one got on deck in the morning to see scores of them on the quay loaded with barley, six sacks on each camel, three on each flank.

It was very interesting to see the camels come up to the ship's side and go down on their knees without any attention. The dockers relieved them of their loads as soon as they were knelt down. Then the beasts got up and gave themselves a good shaking. So it went on all day, or until all the camels had dropped their loads.

I used to be up pretty early in the morning being the cook and steward. But a Maltese chap on the quay with his little hut about the size of a sentry box was doling out hot coffee and rolls before I had the galley fire alight. So I was able to have a little local refreshment before I started work. How the man did it I could not make out, for all the rolls he sold were made on the spot in his little hut and baked in a sort of charcoal oven.

There was a very heavy duty on coal there and it appeared very strange to see liveried officers taking charge of the working of the cargo. At the finish of the day's work every little bit of coal was swept up and the hatches put on and sealed down. You'd have thought it was a cargo of gold instead of coal!

Nearly all the dockside work in Smyrna was done by Maltese and Arabs. There were very few Turks employed there. I noticed that the habits and customs of the people there were very different from what they were in other countries I have seen. For instance, everybody seemed to have their meals outdoors. There were restaurants ashore about 20 yards from the quay and at mealtimes you would see small tables and chairs being brought out and placed in position with charcoal stoves and hubble-bubbles between each two tables. (The hubble-bubble is the pipe they smoke from with a very long stem and which stands on the ground.) The waiters had a very busy time of it, especially during the dinner hour. No traffic was allowed to go on during mealtimes.

One day while I was taking a ramble in the town I came across a fruit-packaging warehouse. I got permission to go through some of the packing rooms or departments. I was very much struck with the cleanliness of everything, especially the fig-packing department. It was white tiled from ceiling to floor and the floor was paved with something like white plaster, only very much harder. The room that I was looking over was about 50 feet long and 20 wide with two sets of tables running the whole length of the room. At each table sat two men dressed in white overalls with piles of boxes on one side of them and a bowl of figs on the other. Each fig was taken and flattened out with fingers and thumb before being placed in the box. A bowl of water for rinsing their fingers stood in the middle of each pair's table.

The men were kept supplied with figs by little girls, also dressed in white, who removed the packed boxes, taking them to another department to have the covers nailed on. There were also a lot of crystallised fruits being packed in the same warehouse in a different department.

They had a strange way of doing their business. After everybody had finished work the tables and chairs were brought out in front of the restaurants and the space between the tables and the quay was given over to itinerant tradesmen of all sorts and the general public who wore very fantastic clothes, some being very picturesque and smart, both male and female, the girls – what I would call "flappers"[2] – wearing their hair in two long plaits.

The restaurants combined general shopkeeping with their other business. I went into one and called for a drop of Scotch whisky. Instead of having it measured out to me, the bottle was placed on the counter with water and a glass for me to help myself. The whisky was a well-known brand called Teacher's Highland Malt which I paid for to the value of fourpence in English money represented by what appeared to be pieces of tin, but what metal it was I cannot say.

The Turkish authorities seemed to be very strict on the shopkeepers regarding weights and measures, for I saw an officer come into the place where I was having the whisky and pick up a loaf of bread and weigh it without so much as speaking or taking notice of anybody. He did the same with several other things that were sold by standard weight then walked out after making a few notes in a book.

The shop assistants and waiters, who are mostly Maltese, all seemed to be able to talk in several languages. They spoke English like natives.

All round Smyrna is lovely country. Fruit of all kinds was growing to perfection and was sold very cheaply. A bushel basket of grapes – fine, big, luscious ones – you could have for a shilling; melons of about seven pounds weight for fourpence. I don't think they were to be obtained anything like that in size, quality or at such prices in England. The insides of the melons were a deep pink colour and all juice. A splendid fruit for hot climates, to be sure. Date palms were also very plentiful as well as figs.

The meat I had to cook was very poor stuff, though. Camel I believe it was. Anyway, it was mostly bones about a yard long with very little meat attached to them and it took hours to cook.

---

2   Girls who defied convention and literally let their hair down were called "flappers" after the motion of their unbridled tresses. The term is most often associated with the jazz and jitterbug set of "bright young things" in the 1920s, when these memoirs were written, although this slang word dates back to the beginning of the century.

16

In journeyings often, in perils of waters,
in perils of robbers,
In perils by mine own countrymen, in perils
By the heathen, in perils of the city,
In perils in the wilderness, in perils in the sea,
In perils among false brethren.
— 2 CORINTHIANS 24

The great drawback to Smyrna was that, although it was such a fine place and the country around so beautiful, you dared not go very far from the town, be it ever such a fine night, on account of the brigands. Nobody was safe from them after dark. They never seemed to trouble about the authorities, for they would come into the town and swagger along the streets with the general public of an evening, speaking to no one and armed to the teeth.

The excisemen having weighed every ounce of coal and the hold having been thoroughly cleansed, we started to load barley, all of which was brought alongside by camels. The freight for barley sent to the United Kingdom at that time by sailing ships was two and sixpence per ton higher than that sent by steamers. I believe this was on account of the sailing vessels always giving delivery of the grain in better condition.

There was one thing that was very cheap and as good as it was cheap in Turkey: that was tobacco. When going the rounds of the bazaar I came across the tobacco department where they were making cigars and cigarettes as well as cutting tobacco. This was packed as it was cut by the boys who, I should say, had just left school.

The tobacco was cut in a very primitive way. They had a board that was hollowed out on the top side on which the tobacco was laid. There was a kind of chain that was worked to bring the tobacco forward to cut it. It was then pressed down by the man's knee to keep it steady for the knife. It was something like the machine I had seen chaff cut with when I was a boy. So you could have your tobacco cut out of any of the samples that were being used at the price of eightpence a pound.

All being ready, we set sail for home, Falmouth being our destination to await orders. When we got out into the harbour and were letting the sails loose the man at the topgallant sail had a bit of a fright, for as he was letting the bunt drop, out fell a whole family of black rats.

They must have made their home in the sail almost as soon as we got into port. There were about a dozen of them and they had made "feathers and down" of the sail. We happened to have a dog and a cat aboard and they managed to kill some of them, but I think most of them got away over the side and made it ashore. Anyway, we did not see any more black rats when we were at sea.

With fine weather and a fair wind we managed to get through the archipelago without any of the disturbances we had on the passage out. I mentioned about the captain being a little bit touched. Well, we were going to see some of his antics.

We were passing Pantellaria in the Sicilian Channel and the skipper was having a good look at the shore through his glasses. All at once he caught hold of the cat which had just come up to him to rub its sides against his leg and sat down on the main hatch to pick the fleas off it. After he had been occupied at that for a quarter of an hour or so he gets up and throws the hapless animal over the side crying:

"Man overboard!"

Of course, we all made a rush for the davits to lower the boat when the skipper shouted:

"Back the topsail and pick up the cat!"

We were not long in obeying his orders, only too glad to know it was just the cat and not one of the crew in distress. We had a good laugh over the trick the skipper had served us, though it was no laughing matter to delay the ship with such foolhardiness. Nor was it, presumably, appreciated by puss.

We were off Cape de Gata[1] on the Spanish coast when the wind dropped and we had to stay there, as it happened, for three whole days. The sea became covered with some kind of weed which gave it a red appearance. I never saw anything like it before. However, we did not stay there without another little diversion, the skipper having one of his fits again.

The watch were all standing about for'ard and not having much to do when he comes along with the dog and the cat and a piece of rattling line. With this he ties their tails together and flings them across a line fastened to the foremast and the rigging.

While he stood and laughed at their antics it was not long before the poor dog was bleeding and making a pitiful howling as, of course, he was no match for the cat under such conditions. After the skipper had seen what his frolic was likely to lead to he went aft, telling the watch to cut them down.

The next day being very hot and still a dead calm we had something happen which gave us all a great shock and made us feel as though our end had certainly come. Just

---

1   Ironically, Cape [Cabo] de Gata translates as Cape of the Cat. Perhaps this inspired the captain's cruel practical joke at the expense of the hapless ship's cat.

about sunset in the first dog watch [4 p.m. to 6 p.m.] we saw a big tramp steamer about a quarter of a mile off making directly for us. And there we were, absolutely helpless. It being the dog watch all the crew happened to be on deck.

Still the tramp continued her course. In the meantime we had got all the pots and kettles as well as the fog horn and bell to make as much noise as possible to get the great lumbering thing to alter course. It was not until she was about half her length off that she did so. We were all shouting and making no end of a noise at her as she passed us, clearing our side by about six yards. During all this time not a soul could we see on her decks.

That was a terrible few minutes, I can assure you. For had we been run down there is no doubt but that would have been the last of the crew and ship which would have been posted at Lloyd's[2] as "missing" and that would have been the end of her. Now, in the old sailing ship days such a thing as one ship being run down by another was almost impossible, especially in broad daylight and in the absence of fogs. For there was always a crew at work either aloft or on deck, as well as the man at the wheel who always steered in the open and not boxed up the same as in the present steamship[3] days.

On the third day of our compulsory three days' rest we had another very great surprise, but one in which there was no danger. It was about sunset and as the sun was going down a grand sight sprang up right ahead of us. It was like a page out of *The Arabian Nights*, so gorgeous was it. It appeared like a great castle of gold. I thought it must have been Ceuta with Europa Point, Gibraltar, in the background. It certainly was magnificent. The skipper had a few anxious moments, not being certain whether it was land or not, for there was no doubt of our being off Cape de Gata nearly 200 miles east of The Rock.

After all the uncertainty and bother the sun went down and our enchanted citadel disappeared. It was another fantastic mirage, but to make doubly sure where we were the skipper ducked below for his quadrant and had his position made certain by the north pole star. Whether such a grand sight has been seen by any other seagoing folk I don't know, but certainly they would not be likely to see such a thing more than once in a lifetime, I'll be bound.

Next morning a breeze sprang up from the east and we were able to continue our voyage. While we were making for Gibraltar we sighted a brigantine on the weather bow. The wind had now veered right round from east to west, so we had a head wind instead of a fair one. I mention this because I want to show what a smart little craft I was aboard.

Now, the vessel we had sighted on the bow was just visible at eight bells in the evening [8 p.m.]. By the same time next morning our positions were reversed, which means we had made almost a true course with a head wind, a thing that very few yachts

2   Edward Lloyd supplied shipping information to interested persons from 1688 in his London coffee house. *Lloyd's List*, a daily publication of shipping news, followed.

3   Tom cannot conceal his distaste for steam vessels.

– if any – could do. By the time we sighted Gibraltar the wind had got round to the south-east and was blowing fairly strong. With all sail set we went through the Strait with a rush and were abreast of Cape Trafalgar the same time next day, which was very good work. We had a fair wind and it did not take us long to get across the Bay of Biscay. We sighted The Lizard about four days after leaving Gibraltar, after which within the next 24 hours we were safely at anchor in Falmouth harbour to await orders.

What a splendid harbour is Falmouth! I have often wondered why the big passenger liners do not make it a port of call, but I suppose Plymouth has the advantage of being so much nearer the metropolis, hence the preference.

After lying at Falmouth for two weeks we learned the cargo of barley had been bought by Guinness, of Dublin, for the brewing of their stout. So it was up anchor and sail for that port where we arrived about 10 days after leaving Falmouth. As soon as the hatches were off I was rather amused to see the number of men who came aboard to take samples of the cargo, each having two sample bags. As there were six men and each bag held about seven pounds the consignees were getting a considerable lot of the cargo free, the above procedure going on for two days.

It was rather interesting to see the way they drew the samples. They had a kind of boring apparatus with which they drilled down through the grain, bringing up about a quart volume of it at each operation.

After seeing the grain discharged I could quite understand why the sailing ships got a better freight than the steamships, for there was not a bushel of the whole cargo out of condition, whereas with the steamships it is very often the case that most of the grain near the boiler is spoiled by the heat.

As the skipper had his wife aboard, he asked me to stay by the ship until he was ready to sail her off again. This I readily did, for the lady was really ill and ought never to have joined her husband on the trip to Dublin from Falmouth.

The skipper told me the ship would be going to Newport to load as he had a very good freight offered him for Terceira in the Western Islands and wished me to join up again, but I told him it was too short a trip and no money to speak of at the end of it as a result. I am sorry to say it was his last voyage, for on his homeward passage the ship struck some rocks near Gibraltar and became a total wreck, the skipper being one of those to lose their lives.

Chapter 16

Falmouth, the harbour Tom Sullivan hails as "splendid"
(courtesy of National Maritime Museum, Greenwich, London)

17

And not by eastern windows only,
When daylight comes, comes in the light,
In front the sun climbs slow, how slowly,
But westward, look, the land is bright!

— **Arthur Hugh Clough**

I now came on to Bristol again after a while and, being very short of money, had to look out for a ship which I managed to get after being ashore about two and a half months. She was the 198-ton brigantine the *Mary Johns* hailing from the same port as the schooner I left in Dublin and which was lost off Gibraltar.

The *Mary Johns* was 115 feet in length with a 24-foot beam and was built at Hayle by Harvey's in 1868. The skipper and owner was Captain Henry E Jacobs. The ship was going to Cardiff to finish loading, having already taken in a quantity of general cargo such as iron rails, puncheons of lime, cement and various other goods. The reason the lime was put in puncheons was that after they were emptied, the sugar refiners used them for filling with return cargo.

All the crew were shipped in Bristol – I signed on on 5 February 1884. So, after lying in Cardiff for about a fortnight we set sail at last for Barbados in the West Indies with a fair wind behind us. Our two weeks' wait was rather a long time and was caused by the difficulty of getting under the loading tips, there being so many big tramps in front of us.

I seemed rather unfortunate regarding my westerly voyages in some respect. Most seemed to be taken on in the winter, and though to get to the end of the present one we had to sail in a much warmer latitude, we had a nasty spell of bad weather in the Bay of Biscay before we met with the North-East Trade Winds. It took quite a fortnight to get out of the bay. Strange as it may seem, there was a fair wind blowing all the time, but as it was quite a heavy gale the skipper-owner would not take any risks, so we hove to until the weather got a bit better.

It was when we were thus weathering out the gale that we found a bad leakage. The ship was making a lot of water and the pumps had to be kept going to keep the water down. You see, there was a great danger of it reaching the casks of lime that were in the bottom of the hold. If it did, there was no knowing what might happen.

We found out about the source of the trouble this way. One day, as the after-guards were having their dinner, the mate thought he could hear water coming in through the stern somewhere and after listening for some time he located the leak which happened to be under the ship's counter: that is, the part of the stern just above the waterline. So every time *Mary Johns* dipped her posterior in the briny, the water soaked through her petticoats with a rush.

While the vessel had been in port before sailing she was on the gridiron[1] undergoing some slight repairs, the stern being part of what had to be overhauled. Well, the carpenters cleared four seams ready for caulking and must have forgotten to do it. So we went to sea with those seams wide open to the elements. It was very fortunate that the leakage was above the waterline, for if it had been below it we should have had a constant influx of water without any chance of stopping it.

Although it was bitterly cold so far as the wind was concerned, the sea was quite warm as we were fortunate enough to sail into the Gulf Stream and were able to wash the decks with the warm water – a very rare thing, I can assure you. There was enough heat in it to melt and wash away all the ice that had frozen on the fo'castle deck.

The weather having improved, the skipper put the ship on her course – the wind still being fair – and took us into the Trade Winds where we were sure of fine weather for at least a fortnight. This gave the skipper a good opportunity to get done what work was necessary, such as unbending the winter sails and replacing them with the summer ones. There were also repairs to the rigging to be done as it had got into rather a bad state. The ratlines especially were in need of attention. Most had to be renewed. Painting the vessel was left until we were on the passage home.

I believe it was the custom on most sailing ships in those days to do at sea all that was necessary in the way of repairs and maintenance as it saved the owners a lot of expense in time and labour in port. You see, the captains could keep those on duty on deck in their afternoon watch to get the work done without the men being able to demur. But in our case on this voyage we did not mind as the skipper was very good and always rewarded us with a tot of rum at eight bells when the first dog watch was set [4 p.m.] and the afternoon watch was going below.

It is these latitudes that you can always catch plenty of fish, mostly bonito and dolphins.[2] Bonito are about the size of a large mackerel and very excellent eating, but to catch them the ship must not be travelling more than four knots. Flying fish used to

---

1   A gridiron in this case was a heavy framework of beams in parallel open order used to support a ship in dry dock.

2   Maybe seafood was seafood to Tom the cook, but dolphins are mammals, not fish, of course!

come aboard without any catching, especially at night. They used to rise out of the water in shoals something like a flock of birds, and the vessel being low down – not more than six or seven feet from the water – a large number used to fall on our deck. Sometimes they would even hit the man at the wheel. Many a good breakfast we had off flying fish, which were about the size of pilchards.

I must mention here one of the little troubles that occur sometimes on board ship. As I was cook and steward, I naturally had to see to it that the crew's meals were ready on time. But one morning, just a few days before we got into port, I had cleaned a lot of flying fish which had flown aboard during the night when my galley stove "mutinied" and – try how I would – I could not get it to do the cooking. Meanwhile, there was the watch below waiting for their breakfast. It did not take them long to let me know it, too, but while they were flinging a few choice adjectives at me, I thought to check the galley fire funnel. So climbing on the roof of the galley I took the top of the funnel off and found it was choked with soot.

"All right, boys," says I. "I've found out the trouble and you shall have your breakfast in a brace of shakes."

So I managed it this way. The watch that had to go below were to have their breakfast first and the other watch were to have theirs when they came on deck, coming into the galley to fetch two at a time (there were only four of them).

I went down to the fo'castle and explained matters which they took quite good-humouredly, saying:

"That's all right, cook. We know it was not your fault."

I think it was the nice lot of fish I cooked for them that clinched smoothing matters over.

They were not at all a bad lot of chaps and were always willing to do anything for me. Sometimes I used to make them dry 'scouse for their tea out of what meat they had had left over from their dinner, or some fishcakes for their breakfast. The dry 'scouse – properly called lobscouse – was made with crushed biscuits and chopped meat, the biscuit being mixed with some of the galley fat, or dripping, and baked in the oven to a nice brown,

"Now, cook," they would say when they thought there was a chance of something extra for breakfast or tea. "Don't you trouble about chopping the meat or boning the fish as the case may be, we'll do that for you."

It was rather amusing to see them hovering round the galley about three o'clock when they knew I was in the habit of having a cup of coffee to see if there was a chance of getting a drop, which they generally did.

We were now nearing our destination and – as usual – started to get things ready for discharging our very mixed cargo. So one fine morning found us in sight of Barbados and I suppose the pilots must have been on the lookout, for they were alongside us about five miles out and one was put aboard without any shortening of sail. There were about half a dozen pilots in the boat, so it seemed they were expecting more shipping in addition to us as they made sail out to sea instead of returning to port in company with our ship.

It is astonishing how very clear the water is in the West Indies. You could see the bottom of the sea outside Barbados quite plainly. The white and pink coral and brain stones[3] all looked very beautiful; the depth of the water was about nine fathoms.

The island, like all the rest of the West Indies, seemed to be extremely well cultivated. Coffee and sugar were the principal articles grown there. Cocoa is also grown to some extent and any quantity of fruit of all kinds. The women and children all seemed to be very busy making copra: that is, scraping the flesh off the inside of the coconut into tubs to be taken out and laid to dry in the sun. When sufficiently dry, it is put into bags for export under the commercial name of copra, or desiccated coconut.

We were about a month in Barbados altogether, having to wait some time after discharging to see if there was any chance of a return freight. But as the broker could not provide one, the skipper thought we would go farther afield. So, leaving Barbados we set sail for Demerara to see if we might fare better there.

A couple of days later found us in Georgetown, Demerara,[4] where we anchored in the river. The first thing the skipper did when we got into port was to try to get the stern made tight. He had failed to get anyone to do it in Barbados, so had to wait until we reached Demerara where he was able to get a ship's carpenter to do it without any trouble, he being a boat builder. Only after his inspection did we find out the full extent of the cause of the leakage.

The skipper went ashore the next morning to look up the brokers. He came back aboard at midday with the news that he had got a freight for the United Kingdom to Falmouth for orders.

When we got into the Demerara River we noticed a fine, full-rigged ship with painted ports – a vessel of about a thousand tons, I should think. As I was rather surprised to see such a vessel I asked the skipper, after he had been ashore, what she was doing there. It appeared she was one of a fleet belonging to a London firm and carried no cargo but was fitted up solely for carrying coolies to and from the West Indies who were engaged to work for so many years. This ship was now taking the returning coolies aboard, another ship being expected every day with a fresh "cargo".

There were also two more vessels lying in the river in which I was very interested. They were two barques flying the German flag, so I asked the carpenter what they were doing there.

"Oh, they are regular traders from Germany with beet sugar and are waiting for their cargoes to be sold," says he.

It appeared that the firm of German refiners who ship most of this beet sugar in

---

3   Coral whose surface looks like the surface of the exposed brain.

4   Georgetown is the capital of what was British Guiana before becoming Guyana on independence on 26 May 1966. Demerara, which gave its name to the brown sugar exported from the area, is the river on the south of which Georgetown lies.

the West Indies have a large fleet of ships which carry nothing else. It is consigned to the various plantations from Cuba in the north to Demerara in the south for blending purposes and then the resultant mixture is shipped again as "pure" Demerara, or West Indies sugar. I wonder what the British housekeeper would think if she knew what she was getting when she asked for Demerara sugar?[5]

The perpetration of this fraud was made possible by the Free Trade Acts and eventually ruined the West Indies sugar trade altogether. The cargo we were going to ship was supposed to be raw sugar and pure cane, but it was anything but that, being of a fine golden colour instead of a darker brown as most raw sugar ought to be.

---

[5]   J.H. Clapham, Professor of Economic History at King's College, Cambridge, around the time these memoirs were written, published a book containing an account of an added refinement, as it were, to maximise the profit from sugar cargoes.

Speculators bought "arrivals" – that is, cargoes of sugar and many other important commodities – sight unseen while still at sea and sold them on at profit before they had even arrived in port. Cargoes would be sold on up to four or five times before landing, each time for an extra mark-up.

Thus the writer's hypothetical housekeeper was not only getting adulterated sugar, but getting it at a price inflated by the "market force" of middlemen's profiteering.

18

An' it all goes into the laundry,
but it never comes out in the wash,
'Ow we're sugared about by the old men
That 'amper and 'inder and scold men.

— **Rudyard Kipling**

The usual custom when a ship gets into port is for the skipper – when he gets ashore – to send someone aboard for his laundry. So one morning, on coming out of the cabin and going to the galley, I found a young darkie lady sitting there and looking quite at home.

"Hullo, Queenie," I says. "Have you come aboard to take up my job, or have you a trade of your own you've a mind to ply among us lonely sailor boys?"

"No, cook," says she with a coy look out of the corner of her big brown eyes. "I come for de captain's laundry work."

"Well, missy, as the skipper is not on board at present, it's only polite I should introduce you instead to his colleagues who reside in what we call the fo'castle as this here galley is no place for a lady."

With that I bowed her out of my domain and led her for'ard where the crew were taking their ease. Our guest giggled at the sight of such strapping lads and was soon invited to sit on their laps, turn and turn about, as they explained to her:

"There's no seating more fitting for a lady such as yourself in our cramped quarters than that afforded by our seamen's knees!"

Then there was such a romp as brought squeals of jollity from all and sundry. And as one thing led to another, it was not only the skipper's linen that got an airing that day! My unexpected introduction of female company to the crew added in no small measure to my popularity, I can tell you.

When the fun had died down a bit, I armed the somewhat breathless ebony beauty along the deck to the cabin. I took her down into it and made her comfortable in an armchair where she proceeded to smooth her rumpled clothing and pat in place her dishevelled hair while waiting for the skipper.

I left her and carried on with my galley tasks, so I know not what passed between her and the skipper in the matter of the cost of cleaning his clothes that time. The crew were adamant they had paid not a penny for the pleasure of our saucy laundry maid's company and I can only guess she made up what deficiencies she might have been owed by adding to the captain's laundry bill. For her willing ways suggested plainly she was no stranger to supplementing her washerwoman's wage by earnings from more exotic dealings with seafarers.

We now started to load our cargo. The stevedores who had charge of the dockers were quite an overbearing lot and thought themselves of great importance, putting on any amount of "side". You would have thought they were the merchants, the way they spoke to the dockers.

It appeared that the skipper agreed to let them have their meals aboard, so when they turned up at dinner time and came to the galley for their dinner, I – of course – gave them the same as the crew were getting, being roast pork, yams and pumpkin pie. But they flatly refused it, saying they were to have the same meals as the ship's officers.

"Well," I says sternly, "you'll have to wait until the captain comes aboard as I have no instructions as to your having any meals aboard."

So when the captain came aboard I asked him if what the stevedores demanded was correct.

"Oh, yes," he says. "I made that arrangement with the shippers so that they should not go ashore and delay the loading."

I then asks: "Are you going to have them in the cabin, then, to have their dinner with you? Because I'm certainly not going to have them in the galley."

"Oh, no," says he. "They must have it anywhere on deck they can fit in."

Which they did, but they had the same menu as the officers nevertheless.

There was one very bad habit which the dockers had: that was stealing anything they could lay their hands on, especially knives and pipes, and also tobacco. If you happened to put anything down in the presence of any of them and looked for it a few minutes after, it was sure to be gone. However, the carpenter who caulked our leaking stern seams was a very good sort of chap as he used to bring me off fruit and an old newspaper occasionally. Sometimes he would give me a bottle of rum, for which I used to pay him with a bottle of fat. So by the time we were loaded I had about a dozen bottles of rum for the passage home.

As we were near finishing loading we were rather surprised to see two of Her Majesty's naval officers come alongside and hail the ship to know if they might come aboard. So as I was standing by the rail I sang out to the skipper – who was still aboard at the time – telling him there were some of Her Majesty's officers wanting to see him. So for'ard he comes at a spanking trot to see what the trouble might be.

"Good morning, captain. May we come aboard?" sings out one of the young fellows. They were both laughing at the skipper as he looked somewhat concerned as to the motive for their visit.

"Oh yes. By all means," says the skipper, all a-fluster. So they comes aboard and, after a hearty handshake, accompanies him down to the cabin.

After being down below about half an hour, they all three came up looking very pleased with themselves. They told the skipper that they were going home for their holidays and had decided to make their passage by a sailing vessel if possible instead of a mail boat and thought that his vessel was the very thing if he would consent to take them, which he did … at less than half the mail boat fare.

Where they were to sleep was not mentioned yet.

I was busy in the galley roasting some cocoa beans when they came along and informed me that they had to be aboard in a fortnight, at which time the skipper had told them he expected to be ready for sea.

No doubt the reader (if I should be fortunate enough to get any) will wonder how I came to be roasting cocoa beans. Really, I was frying them. The crew had asked me if I could get some cocoa as it would make a change from coffee. So, as the skipper was agreeable, I got some, but as it was quite green from the tree it had to be boiled, fried and baked to get the fat out of it before it could be ground in a coffee mill. Although prepared in such a crude manner it was, when all was said and done, cocoa!

I had rather a fright one morning when returning from shore with the day's provisions. For the tide was dead against me and running very strongly. Try as hard as I would, I could not make the ship and as I was getting tired out I hailed her for help. I was answered by one of the crew, a German, who happened to be standing by the galley. He quickly threw me a rope which I managed to grasp and I was soon aboard.

This same German was one of the best men I ever sailed with. A big, burly fellow about six feet tall and with heavy, broad shoulders, he was as good-tempered as he was big.

"Zat voz a close shave, cook," he says as I got aboard. I thanked him for coming to my rescue and added:

"Yes it was, Hans. For I was tired out."

"Vot haf you got for dinner, cook?" he asks, as he looks in my basket.

"Well, there's a little piece of pork, a big piece of pork, a piece of pig's cheek and another piece of pork. What d'ye think of that, Hans? Now go and tell the crew."

And away he went trying to say what I had told him.

"Vun leetle piss of pork, vun big piss of pork, a piss of pig's keek and vun uzzer piss of pork."

As he said it out loud going along the deck the crew burst out laughing, poking fun at him all the time and he, being a good-natured fellow, joined in even though the laugh was against himself.

As we were now loaded and would be sailing in a few days, I thought it advisable to see the skipper about the passengers he was going to carry. So I went aft and asked him what he was going to do regarding the young men. Where were they going to sleep and what was to be their general accommodation on board?

"You, captain," I begins, "have taken the passengers on without thinking of knowing where to berth them as there are no extra berths. Moreover, it is two extra mouths to feed as well as two more to be looked after."

So he put on his thinking cap and, after a bit, he suggested that they should have my berth, which was a double one, the same as his own.

I thought that was rather cool to say the least and told him so, adding:

"And where do you propose that I should sleep? There are no extra bunks in the fo'castle."

"Oh," he says, as smooth as you please, "You can sleep in the sail locker."

"And who, may I ask, is going to pay me for the extra work that I shall have to do?"

"Well, perhaps we had better wait and see what the young men have to say."

I do not know if the captain was aware of it, but to carry passengers without a licence in those days was quite illegal. You could give them a passage, but not make any stated charge. So if I mentioned the circumstances at the shipping office when being paid off there would be trouble for somebody! As I did not wish to do anything of that kind I thought it the wisest plan to come to some understanding beforehand. But I could not get the skipper to have anything more to say about the matter until the passengers came on board.

That time came the day before we left port when the two came aboard and made their way aft. They had a fair amount of luggage, a lot of it being presents including a couple of parrots. There were also two very large trunks, so I called Hans to come and get it all down to the cabin which was no easy matter, the companionway being just wide enough to allow them to be got down. And when they were down they occupied half the cabin floor. So whatever they were paying for their passage, the pair certainly had their fair share of the accommodation in the cabin.

They gave Hans half a dozen plugs of tobacco for his trouble and inquired where the skipper was.

"He'll be here in a few minutes," I tells them. With that he comes aft and we go below to settle matters.

They did not have much to say to the skipper, at least not while I was present, but turned their attention to me as he left the cabin.

"You know, steward, we are having a holiday of six months' duration – the first for as many years we have been serving in the West Indies – and we thought it would be much pleasanter to go home by sailing ship than steamboat. In fact, more like a yachting trip."

"I think you will alter that idea before you get home," says I to myself, adding aloud: "Well, gentlemen, I hope you will have a pleasant passage. I can assure you that I will do my best to make you comfortable, but who is going to pay me for all the extra trouble involved and the giving up of my berth?"

Chapter 18

"Oh," they replies, "the captain will arrange all that as we have paid our passage which is to include everything."

"And am I to be your washer-woman as well?"

They rather smiled at that as though it were a joke.

"Oh no, steward. We have quite enough linen to last three months," they says. "With the exception of table linen, that is!"

As there was nothing very satisfactory in interviewing them, I thought I would have a go at the skipper after the passengers had gone on deck. So I tackled him thus:

"Captain, I've just been having a say to your passengers about who is going to pay me for the extra work entailed by them taking passage in your ship for home, but they referred me to you saying their passage money included everything."

"Don't you worry about that, steward. I will see to that when we get into port."

"Don't forget, captain, that I am giving up my berth and going into the sail locker to sleep to accommodate them, which is not a very pleasant exchange for me."

I was no more successful with him than I was with the passengers, so I gave it up as a bad job, especially as the skipper finished up the argument by saying they would be sure to do the right thing before they went ashore.

So we set sail for Falmouth to await orders.

This being Saturday, I thought I would give the cabin an extra delicacy on the menu for Sunday, having obtained it on the Friday before sailing. The officers and passengers had quite a pleasant surprise when they saw what was laid out for their Sunday dinner. It consisted of roast loin of pork, French beans, sweet potatoes and blancmange. The latter I made from some arrowroot taken from the medicine chest.

"Well done!" says the mate. "I hope you're going to give us a dinner like this next Sunday, steward."

Says I: "I'm afraid you will be disappointed then as there are no shops between here and Falmouth."

We had been out about a week and were getting clear of the Trade Winds, so we had to look out for some rough weather. We were about in latitude 40 degrees north when a gale sprang up from the east and so we had to shorten sail, putting the ship under close-reefed topsail and fore-staysail. She was making rather bad weather of it, shipping some heavy seas, but being a good all-weather ship the seas did not do any damage.

19

Glad did I live and gladly die,
And I laid me down with a will.
This be the verse you grave for me:
'Here he lies where he longed to be;
Home is the sailor, home from the sea,
And the hunter home from the hill.

— **Robert Louis Stevenson**

It had been blowing about three days. Then on the fourth day it blew a bit harder and we were tumbling about a lot. I had just managed to get the dinner down to the cabin – in a bucket – and was coming on deck again.

Just as I got amidships towards the galley a heavy sea struck us and sent the doors of the galley flying, the crew's dinner – it happened to be rice – following into the lee scuppers with the poor old cook close behind.

Oh lor! Here was a fine how-d'ye-do!

The watch could not come to my help for laughing, dinner or no dinner. However, it was not so bad as it might have been as the fire was still going. So after we had picked up the bits and pieces and got the galley a bit straight I got some more rice and soon had their dinner ready again.

We did not see much of the passengers during the heavy weather, they preferring to stay down below out of it.

The weather calmed down a bit the next day after the foregoing fiasco and we came through it without any damage below or aloft. The wind veered round towards the south, so we were able to put the ship on her course and make tracks for Falmouth. I asked the passengers what they thought of their "yachting cruise", as they thought it was going to be.

"Well, steward, to tell you the truth, we would not take another trip like this even if we had it free!"

"I see," I says. "You don't seem to have enjoyed that little bit of a shake-up we had?"

Their silent looks were answer enough.

Chapter 19

At the same time as I was talking to them I noticed they were both cutting up their tobacco on the table and had practically spoiled it – a beautiful, highly polished piece of cabin furniture. I did not say anything to them, but went straight on deck to the skipper and informed him that his cabin table was ruined and that he had better go below and speak to the culprits about it.

"Oh no, steward. I cannot do that myself. You had better talk to them about it as all the cabin furniture is in your charge."

"That's as may be, captain," says I in some heat. "But I cannot make it foolproof and if you don't mind them damaging it, I am sure I don't."

But I did speak to them about it next day and they apologised for being so thoughtless.

We were now getting pretty near our destination and expected to be sighting The Lizard very soon as there were a number of outward-bounders passing us, that being a very sure sign. We made The Lizard 25 days after leaving Demerara and the next day we were in Falmouth harbour. As soon as we were anchored – it being early in the afternoon – the skipper went ashore to see if our orders had come, the passengers going with him to stretch their legs as they said it was not their intention to leave the ship until she got to her port of discharge.

We had to lie at Falmouth for a week before the cargo was sold and then we had to go on to Liverpool. This was another little trip, which the passengers said suited them nicely as they both wanted to get to the North. So we upped anchor and made for our port of discharge. We had just rounded The Lizard when a stiff breeze sprang up from the north-east, increasing to a gale which delayed us quite 24 hours. It took us nearly three days to get to Liverpool.

However, we got there after a good shaking up and were soon made fast to our berth of discharge. I told the passengers the Excise officers would be coming aboard to see if we had any contraband goods and they would have to declare and produce any tobacco they might have as they would not be allowed to take any ashore.

"Oh, we were quite aware of that, steward," they says. "And as we had about two pounds we threw it overboard."

"Well, of all the simpletons that ever came into port, you two are the simplest!" says I. "Why could you not have given it to me and I could have divided it among the crew?"

"We're very sorry, steward, but we never thought of that. However, we have not forgotten you for your kindness in letting us have your berth."

So they handed me all of four shillings.

I thought: "Well, blessed are they who expect nothing, for they shall not be disappointed."

I then did the run to Bristol where on 24 June 1884 I went to the shipping office to get paid off. The skipper asked me if I would make another passage with him, but I had to refuse as I intended to get a berth on shore if possible. So with this, my last voyage at sea before embarking on a life permanently ashore, I must bring my reminiscences to a close, hoping they have been both instructive and amusing, especially to the youths and lads who are still going to school.

The End

Appendix A

A Shellback of the Seventies

Thomas Sullivan Green, alias Tom Sullivan, or Jack Green as he called himself during his career at sea and in later life ashore, did not live to see his memoirs published. However, he did get into print on one occasion, courtesy of the *Bristol Times* newspaper, which published an article about him in its regular Shipping News feature on 29 May 1926, when he was 80 years old, under the heading "A 'Shellback' of the Seventies". It reads:

> *On Monday last we published a notice concerning the current issue of* Sea Breezes, *the house magazine of the Pacific Steam Navigation Company. Special reference was made to the 190-ton brigantine Charles W. Oulton. Our remarks and the quotations from Sea Breezes were read with interest by a local "shellback" of the seventies with whom the writer had the pleasure of conversing yesterday. He is Mr Jack Green, a resident of Southville, who as an ordinary seaman and able seaman sailed the oceans in the seventies when vessels of even 114 tons register were not considered too small for the winter regions of the Atlantic. Mr Green has never "earned a penny in steam"; he is of the days of sail when "sailors were sailors", even though some masters were dubious regarding the identity of the North Star and were known to seek knowledge from the forecastle.*
>
> *Those were the days, too, when they were "dead and buried" only to turn up later in the flesh manning their spick and span little craft which had weathered terrific weather without damage "even to a ropeyarn".*

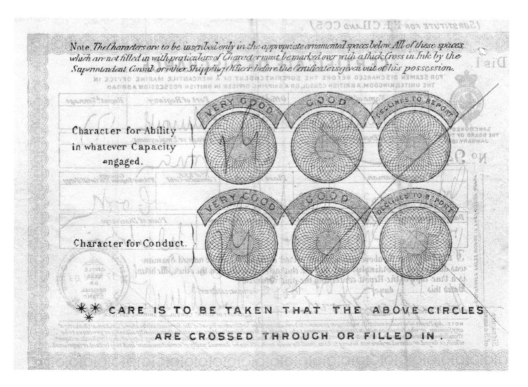

One of Tom Sullivan's certificates of discharge [front and reverse]

Mr Green, despite the efforts of a master of the domestic ship whose one aim in life seemingly was a "clean deck", has managed to preserve a number of discharge certificates all of which bear the two words with a wealth of meaning when paying off and signing on, i.e. "Very Good". These discharges relate to voyages to West Africa in barques Bolivia *and* Lord Duncan *– two names which conjure up visions of Bristol's prosperous past in matters mercantile. They were locally owned by Messrs R. and W. King, of Redcliffe Wharf, when that particular part of the port was busy with trade of a far different nature from that which is carried on there today.*

Other famous old ships on which Mr Green served were the Estephania *(114 tons register), a topsail schooner;* Margaret Ann, *a full-rigged ship;* Sagitta, *a Guernsey brig of 302 tons;* Mary Johns, *a brigantine of 198 tons; and A.D.* Gilbert, *a topsail schooner of 177 tons. The last-named was a Foster-Hain "liner" of the seventies, successors to which are the famous Hain line of "Tre" freighters.*

Mr Green is full of interesting reminiscences of the "good old days". Like most seafarers, ancient and modern, he possesses a disposition of reserve and is disinclined to talk. He promised, however, to meet the writer again and further – and more important – to recount some of his experiences in the Times and Mirror *in the near future.*

That meeting might have taken place, but there is no record of it in subsequent reports in the *Bristol Times and Mirror.*

It is tempting to speculate that the wily old salt's "disposition of reserve" in his interview with the reporter might have been because he had high hopes of his own version of his memoirs being published and did not want someone else to steal his thunder.

Appendix B

Blockade running

Blockade running to supply the Confederate States during the American Civil War was a lucrative, if dangerous, trade for British shipping. Understandably, those who took the risks and got paid handsomely for it were reluctant to acknowledge the fact in the light of the outcome of the conflict when their customers ended up the losers.

Researches have failed to reveal the identity of the West Hartlepool butcher cum ship owner with whom Jack Green signed indentures. However, the following information was published in the *Hartlepool Mail*'s Robert Wood's Notebook on 1 February 1973:

> *The business and diplomatic world generally relies on secrecy when conducting affairs and therefore we are justified in thinking that there was probably much more went on behind the scenes of which we know nothing.*
>
> *Yet in a place like Hartlepool it had always been difficult to keep anything entirely secret. Somebody somewhere knows something and if precise details aren't available, the general shape of things is known by those concerned with such things.*
>
> *In my book* West Hartlepool, *I had this to say of Robert Irvine when writing about his shipyard:*
>
> *Seventy years ago local historians were unable to say precisely when the business of Robert Irvine was established. It was supposed to be some time in the [eighteen] sixties and the founder of the business was said to be concerned in blockade running during the American Civil War.*

It all sounds delightfully vague and so it was intended to be, for when a retired businessman of 80 tells you that in his youth he heard guarded whispers that that was where the money came from with which Robert Irvine started himself in business and that was why he fought shy of the publicity other shipbuilders of the port welcomed, the comments cannot be recorded as history. Yet, knowing West Hartlepool, I could not disregard the tale as idle gossip.

I am still no nearer to proving or disproving the story of blockade running, but I have unearthed, in one way or another, so many links between men called Robert Irvine and the Confederate States and blockade runners that I think the details are worth putting on record. Either the long arm of coincidence has been doing some abnormal stretching or a local shipbuilder had a very interesting family skeleton to hide. Notice I said "men called Robert Irvine" because I have unearthed three who may be entirely separate or they may all be the same man.

In 1858 a Robert Sharp was marine superintendent for the West Hartlepool Steam Navigation Company. In 1872 Robert Irvine was running a shipbuilding and ship repairing business in the Harbour Yard at West Hartlepool. In a Galveston City Directory of the last century we find Robert Irvine running a lighterage and towage business in the port and also a coaling company. In 1862 a report of Lieutenant Colonel Spaight, of the Confederate States' Army, dated September 26, stated that Major J.S. Irvine commanded two armed sail vessels and one steam propelled.

In the same year the Bureau of Ordnance and Hydrography instructed that the Grossetete *and the* Lizzie Simons *were to be armed and Mr Irvine would point out the suitable guns not yet disposed of.*

The Civil War had begun in 1861 and the final hostilities ended in 1865, but there was much more trouble in store for the Confederate States and their supporters when unscrupulous exploiters of the situation came flocking in from the Northern States and the great scandal of the carpet-baggers began.

In those unhappy years those on the losing side who were in a position to do so quit the scene of their operations and departed quietly to set up in business elsewhere as far from the avenging arms of the Northern States as possible. In this connection it is perhaps significant that the first mention of Robert Irvine's ship repairing yard in West Hartlepool occurs in 1865.

Reproduced by kind permission of the Hartlepool Mail.

Appendix C

Execution of William Collier at Stafford Jail

It is not difficult to imagine the horror of witnessing not just a public execution, but a public execution that goes wrong, the condemned man having to suffer the ordeal of being hanged twice before being done to death. The gruesome spectacle made a deep impression on young Jack Green who was only just out of his teens.

He does not dwell on gory details, but conveys the impact of the grisly scene by recalling the "ghastly look" on the victim's face after the hangman's rope broke and he has to wait for another to be put up. Just as telling is the observation of the livid mark left by the first rope before the second is put round the man's neck to finish the fatal job.

I am indebted to Mr Tony Standley, of Stafford, whose knowledge of the history of Stafford Jail has provided the background to the crime which led to this double journey to the scaffold. The man sentenced to death was William Collier, a 35-year-old tenant farmer from the Kingsley area near Froghall, north Staffordshire. Collier was attended by a Roman Catholic priest before his execution and his death must have been devastating for the 12 children he left behind. The large family might have had something to do with the circumstances that led to the capital offence he was tried and sentenced for.

A tenant farmer's earnings at the time must have been spread pretty thin to cover the cost of feeding a dozen hungry young mouths as well as those of Collier and his wife. The temptation for Collier to supplement the family food stocks from the tasty array of local game was apparently irresistible. Records show he had been suspected of poaching on his neighbour's land for many years. Eventually the exasperated neighbour, a well-to-do farmer called Smith, caught Collier red-handed one summer evening in 1866, but he was to pay with his life for making his citizen's arrest. Smith had spotted Collier shooting game with a gun it turned out he had borrowed from another neighbour. Threatened with prosecution by the indignant Smith, Collier panicked and killed him on the spot with a single shot.

The murder investigation got off to a slow start until suspicion focused on Collier when he failed to return the borrowed weapon. Its aggrieved owner was asked if a gun found hidden near the scene of the crime was his. He confirmed it was indeed his and the evidence was thought sufficient to seal Collier's fate. He was tried, found guilty and sentenced to be hanged in public outside Stafford Jail on 7 August 1866.

The executioner was one Smith, of Dudley – no relation to the murder victim. The hangman had achieved some notoriety in the Black Country for the zeal with which he carried out his duties. He served his "apprenticeship" as assistant to William Calcraft, famed for zealous wielding of the noose in London and the Home Counties, where there was no shortage of trade for him. This was a time when a petty theft that a modern magistrate might give only a good ticking off for earned culprits the death penalty.

According to the contemporary account of Collier's last minutes, there was consternation among the crowd when the rope which was meant to part him from his breath slipped and the unfortunate man fell through the open trap to the ground below. Not surprisingly, his legs would not support him as he mounted the scaffold for the second time and he had to be held by the arms to stop him collapsing. For some reason his hands had turned black, the report says. Perhaps his wrists were bound and the circulation had been stopped as he tensed under the strain of his ordeal.

A prison warder fixed the rope to the beam again and this time it did not fail.

There is an intriguing discrepancy between the official version of events of the execution and what is probably the only existing independent eye-witness account; Jack Green's memoirs. The young sailor, whose attention to detail is proved throughout his narrative, describes the rope *breaking*. The official report is careful to record that the rope *slipped*.

If the rope did break the law would have deemed this an Act of God and Collier would have had to have been set free. Perhaps this is why the concerned crowd, including friends and relatives, surged forward when he fell. On the other hand, if the rope slipped it would have been considered an unfortunate mishap and nothing more. In which case – as actually occurred – the condemned man had to be strung up again.

Furthermore Jack Green speaks of two ropes, clearly confirming the breaking of the first one. The official report speaks only of the original rope being fixed to the beam again.

The inference to be drawn from the significant differences in the two accounts is that the authorities were determined that such a long-suspected villain as Collier, who had rounded off an undetected criminal career with that greatest of crimes, murder, was going to pay with his life on the appointed day, come what may.

It was a fairly safe bet for the authorities that the assembled peasantry who witnessed the events that summer day were unlikely to be listened to if any dared to complain about legal niceties being breached as a convicted murderer was sent off to an earlier than expected meeting with his Maker. Even less likely was the chance of any of the rural rabble putting pen to paper to preserve a description of the injustice for posterity. In the event, the calculated risk overlooked the million-to-one chance that a passing young sailor, who happened to be literate, should be in the crowd.

Collier's hanging was the last public execution in Staffordshire. Such ghoulish spectacles were abolished nationwide two years later.

Glossary

AB Able Bodied seaman. One who is able to carry out all the duties of a seaman, able meaning able to "hand, reef (sails) and steer (a ship)". Above Ordinary seaman and below Leading seaman.

abeam In line with the centre of a vessel.

aft In or near the stern (back) of a vessel.

after-guard Men stationed on the quarterdeck or poop to work the sails aft of the mainmast.

aft of Behind.

aloft On or to a higher part of a vessel. Usually up a mast.

amidships In the middle of a vessel.

aniline dye Originally a dye made by distilling indigo with alkali. Also an artificial dye using a colourless oily liquid from coal tar mixed with synthetic pigments.

articles A merchant seaman had to sign articles of employment, which bound him to various merchant shipping Acts of Parliament. His pay and conditions were set, plus the agreement that his captain, the commander of the vessel that was his workplace, was "master under God".

astern Behind or at the back of a vessel. Going astern is reversing.

athwart From side to side or across a vessel.

ballast Heavy material, often stone, gravel, iron, lead, sometimes water, loaded in an empty vessel to maintain stability.

barge A flat-bottomed inland waterway or harbour freight boat into which seagoing vessels' cargo is discharged for onward delivery.

barque A sailing vessel whose aftermost (back) mast carries fore-and-aft sails with square-rigged sails on the other masts (see Figure XX).

beam ends The ends of the cross-beams of a vessel's hull. On her beam ends means on her side, almost capsizing.

below The area of cargo hold or crew accommodation beneath the deck of a vessel.

bend sails To fasten sails to the masts and spars of a vessel.

berth A sailor's sleeping accommodation on board ship. Also, a place in a ship's crew or a quayside mooring place for a vessel.

boarding house Temporary accommodation ashore for the itinerant merchant navy fraternity. Unscrupulous proprietors of these establishments fleeced unwary seamen of their hard-earned wages by advancing loans and giving credit for their board and lodging service, as well as other creature comforts.

boatswain (bosun) A senior seaman, but not an officer, in charge of the sails and rigging, as well as seeing to it that crew members were at their duties.

bolt rope A rope sewn into the edge of a sail to prevent it ripping under strain.

boom A spar, hinged at one end, which is attached to a mast, to which the foot of a fore-and-aft sail is attached.

bow The front of a vessel.

bowsprit A large spar protruding from the bow of a vessel, to which stays are attached. A small sail is sometimes rigged under the bowsprit.

bridge The raised platform or compartment of a vessel from which it is directed by its officers, usually amidships or astern.

brig A two-masted square-rigged vessel with an additional fore-and-aft sail on a gaff and boom from the mainmast.

brigantine A two-masted vessel with a square-rigged foremast and fore-and-aft rigged mainmast.

broach (to) An invariably involuntary action of a vessel, where it is caused to turn suddenly side-on to the wind and waves, usually by heavy weather. In extreme circumstances this can be disastrous, causing swamping or even capsize.

bully beef Boiled or corned beef, providing longer-life meat rations than the shorter-lasting fresh version.

bulwark The part of a vessel's side above the level of the deck.

bunt The middle part of a sail.

cable A strong rope or chain usually attached to an anchor. Also, a nautical length of 200 yards (183 metres).

cannel coal A bituminous coal that burns with a bright flame.

canvas A strong unbleached hemp cloth for sailmaking. Used to describe sails, as in "under canvas" to describe a sailing vessel.

capstan A revolving winch on a vertical axis for winding rope on board ships. Originally man-handled using removable spokes, later versions employed machine power.

caulking Sealing the seams of a ship's timbers by hammering oakum and waterproof material into the gaps.

cheap-Jack A hawker at a fair; used to describe a less-than straight-dealing purveyor of shoddy goods.

clewing up To tie a square sail to its yard arm by the clew, the lower end. This allows the sail to be released again relatively easily if necessary. Furling the sail would see it securely rolled and fastened to the yard arm, needing more work to release it for use again.

clink Dating back to the early 16th century, this slang expression refers to a prison in Southwark, London, and came to be used as a general term for being in custody; "in the clink".

clipper A fast sailing vessel. The term was usually applied to the 19th century's square-rigged merchant vessels used in the tea trade, such as *Cutty Sark* and *Thermopylae*, which raced their cargoes from the Far East to home markets in Britain to command the best prices. Speed was of the essence to offer the first of the season's fresh coveted commodity to a nation that laid great store by the "cuppa".

close-reefed Reefing a sail makes the area it presents to the wind smaller. It is usually achieved by tying it back, often using built-in ropes on commercial sailing vessels. Roller-reefing allows the luxury of being able to use a single, deck-located rope to reduce sail area by winding in the canvas on its spool.

companionway The staircase on board a vessel leading from deck to deck.

coppers Low-denomination pre-decimalisation coins. These were a large-sized penny (12 of which would make the present 5p), a half-penny and a farthing, a quarter of a penny.

copra Dried coconut kernels from which coconut oil is obtained.

davit A crane mounted on board a vessel to hoist objects onboard and outboard.

deckwork Seamen on duty but not needed on sailing work could be employed on maintaining the parts of their vessel among the most exposed to the elements: the deck and the structures it supported. Wood, iron, brasswork and more would need attention. Skippers legitimately used their articled shipwrights for this work, thus saving money for themselves or their owners on work back in port.

discharges   To safeguard owners, skippers, crews and those whose cargoes were carried on merchant vessels, various laws were enacted by the British Parliament to regulate the trade. Among these was a system of assessment for seamen. They had to sign on and sign off from the ships they worked on and their performance had to be set down in writing by their captains. On completing the obligations of his articles of employment on a vessel, a seaman was given a certificate of discharge confirming his competence. These were vital documents for a seaman wishing to sign on for more work at sea.

dogwatch   See **watch**.

doldrums   An area around the Equator notorious for light winds.

doughboy   A boiled flour dumpling.

duds   Slang for clothes.

ebb tide   Falling or low tide in waters affected by tidal flow.

fairway   A stretch of water a vessel may enter in the knowledge that it is safe to do so and that wind and water allow it.

fathom   A measure of depth of 6 feet (1.82 metres).

flood tide   The opposite of an ebb tide. A rising or high tide in waters affected by tidal flow.

fo'csle (forecastle)   Originally the forward castle from which fighting men attacked the opposition. Later this described the home of the crew of a vessel, towards the front, the officers being housed aft (at the back).

for'ard   Towards the front of the vessel.

fore-and-aft sails   Sails that catch the wind along the length of a vessel rather than from behind are fore-and-aft. This is sometimes described as Bermuda rig. It enables sailing boats to sail "close to the wind", meaning they can steer to more points of the compass. Those that take the wind full on are square sails. Square sails narrow the options for what directions can be steered.

foremast   The mast nearest to the front of the vessel.

forepeak   The accommodation for crew or cargo at the forward-most part of a vessel.

foresail   A fore-and-aft sailset on rigging in front of the foremast.

foretopsail   A square sail at the top of the foresail.

furl   To roll and secure a sail after use. On sailing vessels trading across oceans these sails were not only large, but also heavy canvas. Furling them was no mean feat, even in good weather.

gaff   A spar attached to the after-most mast of a sailing vessel and supporting the top of a fore-and-aft sail.

galley   A kitchen at sea.

galiot   A fast single-masted sailing vessel that originated in the Mediterranean and was copied by the Dutch.

gondola   Not just an expensive tourist trap in Venice. Gondolas were boats into which cargoes were discharged from vessels that had brought their bounty from abroad.

halyard   Rope or tackle to raise a sail.

hammock   A hanging bed, made of canvas or rope, suspended between two points in a vessel allowing it to move in unison with the hull.

hand   A member of a vessel's crew.

hatch   An opening in the deck of a vessel to give access to the cargo hold.

hawser   A large rope used to secure a vessel.

headed   When there is a considerable wind shift that curtails a vessel's forward motion, it is headed. An experienced helmsman would anticipate this in normal circumstances, but ships can be headed for many reasons.

headway   A vessel's movement forward; making progress on its intended course.

heave to   To stop a vessel in the water without using an anchor. Sailing vessels heave to by releasing all the ropes (sheets). This spills wind from the sails, curtailing their motive power.

helm   The mechanism by which a vessel is steered.

hold   The area below decks where cargo is stowed.

holystone   Soft sandstone used to scour the wooden decks of sailing ships.

holystoning   The chore seaman were regularly ordered to do to keep the decks of their ships in a gleaming white condition.

hookpot   A pot for food or drink designed to hang from the bars of a galley range on board ship.

hue and cry   An outcry calling for the pursuit of felons.

Ikey   In an era when people gave and took insults without a thought of political correctness, anyone thought to be a Jew might be called "Ikey Mo", a derogatory abbreviation of the two male Jewish names, Isaac and Moses.

Jack o'Lantern   A man with a lantern as a night watchman in the late 17th century; later the term was used to indicate a kind of elusive spirit.

jib   A triangular sail set fore-and-aft at the fore end of a sailing vessel.

jib boom   A spar that runs out from the bowsprit and holds the foot of a sail.

jolly boat   An open boat with sails. A boat should never be confused with its big sister, a ship, in the hearing of an old salt, who will undoubtedly growl: "Boats goes on ships." The only exceptions are submarines, which are designated as boats.

keel   The backbone of a vessel upon which the rest of it is constructed.

keelson   Part of a vessel's structure that joins the keel to the rest of the constructive members of the hull.

knot   A unit of speed at sea, being one nautical mile per hour (85 k.p.h./1.5 m.p.h.). A nautical mile is 2025.4 yards (1.852 km).

lamp-trimming   On board ship oil lamps would have provided light for navigation and for the crew below decks. The wicks of the lamps soon became blackened with burning, which dimmed their light. A quick snip with scissors or a sailor's knife restored the efficiency of the cloth wick, fed by oil from its reservoir by capillary action.

lay up   Whether for repairs, maintenance or other reasons, a vessel might be laid up off the water and thus out of service.

lee   A sheltered area opposite the wind direction.

leeward (lew'ard)   Having a direction away from that of the wind.

lightship   A moored or anchored ship with a light beacon.

Line, The   The Equator.

lock   A system of water-retaining gates to regulate the level and flow of water in a navigable waterway.

log book   The ship's diary; a record of a vessel's progress, as in recording the log of passage through the water, plus other matters relating to the voyage.

longboat   Sailing vessels carried boats aboard which could be sailed or rowed ashore when docking was not possible or required, or between ships in open water. The longboat was the largest of such a craft. Up to 10 metres in length, the longboat would be stowed on deck, between masts.

lying at anchor   Anchored in open water as opposed to being moored alongside a quay.

mainmast   The principal mast on a vessel.

make fast   To secure ropes or a vessel itself for the purpose intended.

mate   An officer under the captain of a vessel, sometimes holding the same qualification but not the experience thought necessary for command. Merchant vessels might have first, second and even third mates. Gold rings on the sleeves of their uniforms denoted their rank. The captain had four rings.

mizzen mast   The mast aft of the mainmast in a sailing vessel with three or more masts.

Mo   This was a reference to the male Jewish names Moses. See also **Ikey.**

navvies   The armies of labourers who dug the network of canals, or cuts, across Britain in the 18th century and beyond to feed the commercial boom that was called canal mania were called navigators. This was because they were making the routes for expanding inland navigation. Their title soon became shortened to navvy and now the term is used to describe anyone who wields a pick and shovel.

navigation – The skill of steering vessels through wind and waves, avoiding obstacles on the way. Some see this skill as imbued with a mystique akin to witchcraft. However, true experts will tell any would-be mariner that navigation is no more or less than a cautious appreciation of all the facts and figures available, coupled with the judicious use of Mk I eyeball.

oakum   Loose fibre obtained by picking apart old rope (see **caulking**). This tedious task was undertaken by Victorian prison inmates. There are those who point to multiple occupancy of modern jail cells as being a backward step from those Victorian houses of correction that only had one man to a cell. This overlooks the fact that the rest of the cell was taken up with machines and materials for enforced labour, such as picking oakum.

overboard   Anything or anyone falling from a vessel at sea is said to have gone overboard.

orders   Vessels reaching the end of a passage with cargo aboard needed to be told to which ports they had to go to discharge. Orders were communicated to vessels by agents for the owners at ports designated for this duty. Falmouth, Cornwall, and Queenstown (Cobh), Eire, were among the busiest.

pannikin   A small metal drinking vessel.

passage   A journey by sea.

pilot suit   Seafarer's clothing of rough, woollen cloth.

pilot   A person with local navigational knowledge authorised to advise sailing masters on how to proceed through waters in their jurisdiction. Signal flag H, with vertical white and red halves, indicates that a pilot is aboard a vessel. This is flown permanently on some short sea crossings, where the skipper is a pilot in his own right.

pipe clay   A fine white clay forming a paste when water is added, used in making tobacco pipes of the kind universally smoked in Victorian times.

pitch pine   A generic term for several species of pine tree that were harvested for their resinous qualities to create turpentine or pitch.

poop   The stern deck of a vessel and that which was the domain of the captain and his officers.

port side   Left.

porthole   Aperture in the side of a vessel, usually glazed.

puncheon   A large cask. It was usually employed for fish or liquids and the capacity varied.

quadrant   A navigational instrument for taking altitude readings of celestial bodies.

quarter   Usually a reference point about a vessel. Anywhere aft of the centre point is referred to as the port or starboard quarter to indicate the position of a point of interest to the observer.

quaterdeck   That part of a ship's upper deck to the stern reserved for officers.

ratlines   Rope fastened horizontally to shrouds in a vessels rigging to act as steps to climb masts.

rattling line   The type of rope used for ratlines.

reef   To reduce the area of a sail by tying part of it off to present a smaller area of canvas to the wind. Roller reefing achieves the same object with less effort, as long as the spooling mechanism does not jam, a fault for which many examples of this labour-saving device were notorious.

register   As in tonnage; the weight of a vessel registered with the shipping authorities.

registry (of shipping)   With vessels plying every ocean, those who invested in such often precarious and uncertain enterprises needed some reassurance. Thus vessels were registered by name and code numbers that could be tracked across the world. Of course, this was not so much to monitor the welfare of the seamen involved in the trade as to keep track of the costly ships and cargo on which investors had risked their money. The system was started in 1688 by Edward Lloyd, who supplied shipping information in his London coffee house. This led, eventually, to the publication of the daily *Lloyd's List* devoted to shipping news.

rigging   Usually applied to ropework but, strictly speaking, descriptive of standing and running rigging. Standing rigging applies to stays, ratlines and the like, with running rigging referring to ropes such as halyards and sheets that are expected to be on the move, or running, as shifts of direction, wind or weather demand.

roads   A sheltered stretch of water where vessels can anchor in safety. Usually near a harbour entrance or river estuary.

rove   To form cotton strands into a fibre called rovings. It should be remembered that the life of a seaman under sail depended on rope of some kind or another.

rudder   A broad and flat piece of metal or wood attached vertically to the stern of a vessel to steer it.

rudder-head   The upper part of the rudder to which steering gear would be attached.

running gear   Ropes, blocks and tackle that have to move to keep the canvas of a sailing vessel presented at the best angle to the winds for optimum speed and course direction to be maintained. The care and maintenance of running gear was a constant chore for crews of deep-sea sailing vessels. Ropework skills were second nature to sailors as part of their everyday working lives, as well as being celebrated by them in decorative work using cordage.

salvage   Compensation paid to those who have voluntarily saved a ship or its cargo from loss at sea or the act of doing so.

sea legs   Sea legs move with the motion of a vessel. Gaining one's sea legs when first setting sail is a polite way of measuring how long it takes for seasickness to be overcome. Not so often remarked upon is how sea legs have to become land legs after some time aboard ship, especially in heavy weather. Sea legs accustomed to the motion of a bucking deck can be unprepared for terra firma, causing unsteadiness of gait, not necessarily the result of a seaman refreshing himself at a dockside hostelry after a stormy voyage.

schooner   A small seagoing sailing vessel with fore-and-aft rigging, originally with two masts, but later with three, sometimes four. The foremast was usually shorter than the others.

scuppers   An opening in a ship's side at deck level allowing water to run away.

shanty   Sailors' song, usually in rhythm with work such as hauling ropes or winding a capstan.

sheet   Rope attached to the bottom corner of a sail, to be adjusted to optimise the sail's attitude to the wind.

shipping office   The official establishment where ship owners or their agents looked for crews for their vessels and where seamen looked to fill the bill.

ship's biscuit   A hard-baked biscuit that was notorious for its resilience, but was, nonetheless, a source of carbohydrate for mariners away from land for many months. Parasites appreciated this and many a sailor had to tap his ship's biscuit on the fo'csle table to evict weevils from their comfy home.

shorten (sail)   To reef sails or furl them up completely, usually in anticipation of stronger winds.

shrouds   Standing rigging of a vessel, usually securing the masts.

sidespring boot   Footwear with elasticated sides. Nowadays, a Chelsea boot.

signal   Ship-to-shore and ship-to-ship communication, which in the days before wireless, let alone the internet, was achieved by physical gesture, semaphore flagging, internationally recognised signal flags and lights. When approaching a reporting port, such as Falmouth, after a voyage, a vessel would "make its number", flying the code signals of its Lloyd's registered number – easier for the spotter ashore than trying to make out the often obscured name on the bow or stern. The number would identify the appropriate agent's orders to the skipper to proceed to a particular port to deliver his cargo. Again, signal code flags would be used to pass this information.

skipper   A ship's captain, universally acknowledged as "Master under God". Most merchant marine masters bore this onerous responsibility with modesty and decorum. However, as Tom Sullivan Green found to his cost, some substituted the "under" for "over" the Almighty.

spar   Any mast, yard arm or boom on a sailing vessel.

square-rigged   A vessel with sails that are set at right angles to the deck of the ship rather than fore-and-aft.

starboard   Right.

stay   A rope, chain or wire that holds up masts.

staysail   A loose-footed sail flown between masts and from standing stays or from forestays. Anything to get more speed out of a merchant vessel to get her cargo to market as soon as possible. The romantic tea trade clippers, dashing in both senses of the word, packed every space possible between masts with staysails to squeeze that extra ounce of speed from their sleek hulls. They even used extensions to their yards to fly stun'sls (studding sails). Stun'sls are often pictured in paintings of these magnificent Formula 1 racers of the seas but, in reality, they were thought more trouble than they were worth by mariners.

stern   The back of a vessel.

stevedore   Person employed to load and unload ships.

stowed   Loaded aboard a vessel.

suit (of sails)   A full set of sails for a particular vessel. Winter and summer suits would be carried by most deep-sea sailing ships. A skilled sailmaker might well be part of a larger ship's crew, but most ABs would have the ability to do running repairs to sails. This was often needed as they were subjected to the worst of weather and had to be made to last to save owners the expense of replacing them.

tackle(s)   As in block and tackle. Systems of pulleys and ropes used to shift heavy weights on and off vessels.

taffrail   The rail at the stern of a vessel.

tide   The alternate rising and falling of the sea level, usually twice in a lunar day at each place, due to the gravitational attraction of the moon and sun. The alternate inflow and outflow are called the flood and ebb, respectively. At times of full and no moon, spring tides occur, giving a range of the highest high tides and the lowest low tides. At half moon, neap tides apply, giving the smallest range of lowest highs and highest lows.

tiller A horizontal bar attached to the rudder-head to act as a lever by which the rudder is moved for steering.

to'gallant (topgallant) An upper square sail, flown below royal sails.

to'gallant fo'csle head A short deck above the upper deck, forward and over the forecastle.

tops'l (topsail) schooner A two-masted sailing vessel with gaff-rigged fore-and-aft sails but two square sails at the top of the foremast.

Trade Winds This originally referred to a wind blowing steadily in the same direction, but came to be more specifically applied to a wind blowing towards the Equator from the north-east or south-east.

tramp A cargo vessel, especially a steamship, taking available cargoes for any port instead of trading between fixed ports.

truck A circular or square wooden cap at the top of a mast or flagstaff, usually with holes for halyards (ropes) to pass through.

tug A small, sturdy boat used to tow larger vessels in and out of docks and harbours.

under way Progress by a vessel on its chosen course.

unshipped Removal of some substantial item from a vessel, as in unshipping a mast.

veer Of a change in wind direction. Direction is described in terms of the direction from which the wind is coming. That is, a westerly wind is coming from the west. If a wind veers, its direction changes clockwise. Thus, a westerly wind will veer northerly. The reverse alteration is known as backing.

watch A ship's crew would usually be split into starboard and port watches. Officers commanding a watch would choose in turn from the recently signed-on crew at the beginning of a voyage. The reason for this was that a trading vessel sailed 24 hours a day and the crew had to be on duty to man her. Dividing the ship's company into watches made this possible. Their hours were laid down in a time-honoured routine. The sailing day started at noon. The afternoon watch was from noon to 4 p.m. Then came the first dog watch, 4 p.m. to 6 p.m., followed by the second dog watch, 6 p.m. to 8 p.m. First watch was 8 p.m. to midnight, middle watch midnight to 4 a.m., morning watch 4 a.m. to 8 a.m. and forenoon watch 8 a.m. to noon. This made seven watches, which the crew kept alternately. The two-hour dog watches made a variation in working hours to vary the routine.

weather To windward of headland or another vessel. In a windward direction. Also, to cope with adverse conditions, as in "weather the storm".

wheel Larger vessels are steered by a wheel. This serves the same purpose as a tiller to move the rudder, but uses systems of pulleys, gearing chain or rope to change a vessel's direction.

windlass A winch for hauling rope or chain aboard ship. Now mechanically driven, windlasses were originally powered by sailors using spokes inserted horizontally into the top of the contraption.

yard arm A spar from which a square sail is set. The yard arm holds the top of the sail, which is adjusted by ropes (sheets) attached to the bottom. Yard arms pivoted around their attachments to the masts in accordance with wind direction and course steered.

yaw For a vessel to deviate temporarily from a course from side to side, often as a result of sudden changes in weather conditions, but sometimes because of helmsman error.

Full Rigged Ship

Three Masted Barque

Brig

Brigantine

Barquentine

Topsail Schooner

Sailing ships' rigging patterns (courtesy of Patrick Starke)

Index